$MART RETIREMENT PLANNING

WINNING STRATEGIES TO BUILD LARGE SUMS OF RETIREMENT INCOME; INVESTING, CREATING PASSIVE INCOME AND MAKING YOUR MONEY LAST A LIFETIME

Noelle Romero

ISNB: 978-1-915217-27-1 (paperback)

Table of Contents

Introduction

Having a secure financial future is important for all of us. That includes having a secure retirement to look forward to. But there's a lot more involved than just putting a bit of money aside. Your retirement might be a long way off – if you're twenty, you've got forty to forty-five years of work ahead of you if you live in the US. You may have up to forty-seven if you live in the UK, since they changed the retirement age recently. It's quite difficult to look that far ahead. You might not even have a clear idea of where your career will have taken you in five years' time.

And retirement isn't a holiday, or a wedding, or paying the deposit on a house, or some other one-off event that you can save a defined amount of money for and know it's going to be enough. You're building up enough investments to be able to pay you an income for the rest of your life. So there's some difficult math to do, and if finance isn't your strong suit, that can be a barrier to understanding.

People are living longer than they used to do. In the 1940s and 1950s, very often men retired from work and only lived two or three years after their retirement, particularly if they had done physical jobs like working in a steelworks or a mine. They were worn out and average life expectancies were low. Even in 1971, average male life expectancy in the UK was just sixty-eight; now, it's more than eighty-one. You might easily have twenty to thirty years of retirement to finance.

Besides, the way we live in retirement has changed. If you retire at sixty-five, you'll probably still be active and want to get some fun out of life. You might want to travel, take up a new sport or leisure interest, or perhaps help your grandchildren out with money towards buying a house, funding post-grad studies, or even starting a business. You may think you should get the most out of your money while you're young, but if you end up miserable in your sixties, that might not prove to be the best decision!

Just a few role model retirees I've noted in the past few years:

- Fauja Singh, of *Sikhs in the City* running group, ran his marathon-best at the Toronto Waterfront Marathon at the age of ninety-two. He ran another marathon at 100. No wonder they call him the Turbaned Tornado!
- Harry Leslie Smith became a Twitter sensation in his eighties, raising money to help refugees.
- Devanshi Mavani had just retired from her accountancy career when she was diagnosed with Type 1 diabetes. So she climbed Kilimanjaro. Now she's heading for Machu Picchu and the Inca Trail.
- Mary Dickins became a performance poet at sixty-two and discovered silliness, anarchy, and fame.

(If you want to read some more inspiring stories, The Guardian's "New Start After 60" series is quite fascinating).

Of course, in your later years, you may end up with some major healthcare expenses. Minor healthcare expenses, such as upgraded eyeglasses or extra vitamin supplements, can also take a nibble at your monthly income.

Or you may just find aches and pains are an issue, in which case you may decide it's worth paying for a little extra comfort. Backpacking as a sixty-five-year-old is different from backpacking in your twenties, though some eighty-year-olds are still happy using 'youth' hostels. So even if you're reasonably healthy, life can cost a bit more.

Don't rely on the government to bail you out. Social security in the US will only pay around $1,700 a month; in the UK, the basic state pension is less than £1,000 a month. That's not going to pay for any luxuries. Most

Americans spend $3,900 a month on basics, more than twice the social security payment.

Many new retirees are disastrously poorly prepared for their retirement. A 2019 report from the Economic Policy Institute showed that most Americans aged fifty-six to sixty-one had just $21,000 in their retirement accounts (that is, in 401(k) plans). In thirty years, that's all they had saved. Thirty-two- to thirty-seven-year-olds had, on average, just $1,000, which means they already missed the boat.

Admittedly the 401(k) is only one way of saving for retirement. Some of these youngsters will have money invested in a business which they plan to sell at some point to raise a capital sum. Some people will have an employer-funded pension, though that's becoming less and less common. But they must be in the minority, so many people are badly prepared, and that's a major problem. Even when employers automatically enroll their employees in a 401(k), the amount being saved may not be enough to create a viable pension income on retirement – and because of the sophisticated nature of the calculations involved, many people simply don't know whether or not their plan will deliver.

The question that you should really start with is: "Will my retirement savings allow me to live the lifestyle I want to?" But few people ever get round to asking, let alone answering, this question. You want to have an idea of where you're going, and you want to know whether right now, you're on track to achieve that, or not.

You can start any time. In fact, the younger you are when you start thinking about retirement, the more time you have to save the money you'll need, though most people only start thinking about retirement seriously once they get to their mid-forties.

If you're twenty-something, even saving quite small amounts can make a big difference. In fact, if you're making good money at the start of your career and are able to put money away before you have a family or other commitments, it makes great sense to look at long-term savings for retirement. That's because the earlier you start investing, the longer you have for your investments to grow.

Let's take a simple example of *compounding*. Compounding happens when you leave your returns, as well as your initial capital, invested. For instance, when you leave money in a savings account, you will get paid interest on your money in the first year, but in the second year you'll get paid interest on that money and on the interest received in year one, as well. That keeps rolling on, like a snowball, getting bigger all the time.

Let's imagine you put $2,000 in a bank account aged twenty-five and your interest was 3% a year. After thirty-five years, you would have $5,627 in the account if you kept your interest rolling up. If you took out your interest every year, just leaving the initial payment in the account, you'd still only have $2,000 at the end of that period! If we look at the amount of interest you're getting each year, if you just left the $2,000 there, you'll still be getting $60 a year, just like you did at the start. But if you let the interest roll up, by year thirty-five (aged sixty), you'll be getting $164 of interest. That's a big difference.

And what would happen if you started saving later, with the same amount? If you didn't start saving till you were thirty-five, you'd only have increased your capital to $4,187 by aged sixty, and your interest income would be $122. That's 25% less. And if you hadn't started investing till you were forty-five, you'd only have $3,115 in savings by aged sixty, and you'd get $90 in interest – 45% less. And just imagine if your starting capital was ten times more than $2,000.

But this is a very simple example, based on a single amount paid in. Your pension contributions will keep going into that account over your working life, and you may increase them as your salary increases. You can, to some extent, play catch-up, but the longer you leave it to get started, the higher the later payments will need to be to compensate. So it pays to get started as soon as you can.

Here is a table showing the compounding we discussed above, based on you adding $2,000 in year one and leaving your rolled up interest in the account. The interest amounts are based on you receiving 3% annual interest.

Year	Start of year	Interest earned	End of year
1	$2,000	$60	$2,060
2	$2,060	$61.80	$2,121.80
3	$2,121.80	$63.65	$2,185.45
4	$2,185.45	$65.56	$2,251.01
5	$2,251.01	$67.53	$2,318.54
6	$2,318.54	$69.56	$2,388.10
7	$2,388.10	$71.64	$2,459.74
8	$2,459.74	$73.79	$2,533.53
9	$2,533.53	$76.01	$2,609.54
10	$2,609.54	$78.29	$2,687.83
11	$2,687.82	$80.63	$2,768.45
12	$2,768.45	$83.05	$2,851.50
13	$2,851.50	$85.55	$2,937.05
14	$2,937.05	$88.11	$3,025.16
15	$3,025.16	$90.75	$3,115.91
16	$3,115.91	$93.48	$3,209.39
17	$3,209.39	$96.28	$3,305.67
18	$3,305.67	$99.17	$3,404.84
19	$3,404.84	$102.15	$3,506.99

Year	Start of year	Interest earned	End of year
20	$3,506.99	$105.21	$3,612.20
21	$3,612.20	$108.37	$3,720.57
22	$3,720.57	$111.62	$3,832.19
23	$3,832.19	$114.97	$3,947.16
24	$3,947.16	$118.41	$4,065.57
25	$4,065.57	$121.97	$4,187.54
26	$4,187.54	$125.63	$4,313.17
27	$4,313.17	$129.39	$4,442.56
28	$4,442.56	$133.28	$4,575.84
29	$4,575.84	$137.28	$4,713.12
30	$4,713.12	$141.39	$4,854.51
31	$4,854.51	$145.64	$5,000.15
32	$5,000.15	$150.00	$5,150.15
33	$5,150.15	$154.50	$5,304.65
34	$5,304.65	$159.14	$5,463.79
35	$5,463.79	$163.91	$5.627.70

If you're already investing towards retirement, you want to monitor how you're doing. Are you saving enough? Are you getting a good enough return from your investments? Are you taking too high a risk, or not enough risk? A big advantage of following your retirement savings this way is that when life throws you a curveball, whether that's losing a job, unexpectedly having triplets, or getting posted overseas, you know what you've achieved so far and how much wiggle room you have.

When I started looking at my own pension entitlements a while back, I found that I had a potential gold mine, but that I'd made some really stupid decisions along the way. For instance, I had money in schemes that didn't give me much flexibility and they had missed out on nearly all the stock market gains while I'd been holding them. I had turned down a company pension scheme at one employer, while I was struggling to pay my mortgage in my early twenties on a low salary; I now realize it was one of the best-funded and most generous schemes around. I switched my savings into a new scheme that invested in higher-return assets, since I know I still have years of investing to go. So far, even after a stock market crash, I'm doing much better than I was, and I'm on track to have a great retirement and maybe even retire early. But I really could kick myself for those basic errors.

I found out a lot when I was looking at my own retirement plans and I know how difficult it can be to get on top of things. So I've written this book to explain the basics of retirement planning in everyday language, without small print, and with as little advanced math or jargon as possible. Whatever you're planning for your own retirement, whether it's the snowbird lifestyle with an RV, training as a pilot (one of my best friends' favored retirement activities!), enjoying the French country life or a busy big city lifestyle, let's make it all about *you*.

If you enjoy this book and find it valuable, I would be really grateful if you would consider leaving a review. Your feedback is incredibly valuable and helps other readers discover and appreciate the book and encourages my writing journey.

Chapter One
WHAT DOES RETIREMENT MEAN?

Retirement means many things to different people, but we can simplify it down to a single definition: the stage of life at which you can stop working for a living and live off savings, passive income or a pension. While most people retire at fifty-five or above, it's possible to retire much earlier – that is, to achieve financial independence (that's what the FIRE movement is all about – the Fire movement started in the US but also has a growing fan base in the UK. Its main ideas originate from the 1992 book '*Your Money or Your Life*' by Vicki Robin and Joe Dominguez. The aim is for you to retire before the age of 55 by being frugal, cutting expenses and setting aside a big proportion of your earnings. There are many books on the subject if you're interested in learning more).

For some people, retirement will mean a life of leisure. For others, it may mean being able to pursue a passion rather than having to work to get by. For instance, a corporate executive might decide to quit in their forties to become a jeweler or artist. Some people will retire due to ill health; others may feel burnt out and want to retire early. For most, retirement is a chance to go and do what they want; for many, it frees them up to become more involved with grandchildren and other family members.

However, for this to be possible, there needs to be some financial planning in the background. That might be through a formal pension scheme, like an IRA or 401(k) if you're in the US, or, in the UK, a SIPP, or it might be through other investments. Some people will have an employer-funded scheme. Some will rely on state pensions, though as I pointed out, these are not overly generous. In fact, most people will probably have funds coming from more than one source. For instance, a government employee might have their own pension plan, a government-funded pension, and some stock market investments that pay dividends.

Retirement as we know it now is a relatively new concept that has come about as life expectancy has increased. In many medieval and earlier cultures, those who lived to advanced age 'retired' to spiritual contemplation in a monastery or refuge and those who could no longer work were looked after by their extended families. The UK introduced a state pension in 1909; the US had to wait till 1935 for government-sponsored benefits.

You have a great deal of choice about your retirement. For instance, you'll need to decide:

- When you retire.
- What lifestyle you'll adopt in retirement.
- What that means for how much you'll need to spend.
- When to start taking social security.
- Whether to take a pension lump sum, annuity, or flexible income.
- Whether to choose benefits that will provide for a surviving spouse.

While the standard retirement age is considered to be sixty-five, and that may be specified by your employer, there is no mandatory retirement age in the US. The IRS will generally penalize you for taking retirement payouts before age fifty-nine-and-a-half, though there are some detailed exceptions (such as for military service and disability). But you don't have to take your social security at any particular age; in fact, delaying it allows you to take a bigger pension.

In the UK, employers used to be able to force employees to retire at sixty-five, but the rules were changed in 2012 so there is now no mandatory retirement. State pension age is sixty-five for most who are retiring now, but it's gradually rising and will reach sixty-seven by 2028. That's the age at which you can claim the state pension, though as with the US, delaying your claim may net you a bigger income when you do retire.

When you reach retirement, you've worked your whole life. Now it's time to take a back seat. It may be that you're feeling tired of your work anyway, or you may retire for medical reasons. In most cases, the availability of social security or private pensions is a key determinant in the timing of people's retirement decisions, though if you have substantial savings you can be more flexible.

You go from the six o'clock alarm call to choosing whether to have a lie-in. You can do what you want and go where you like. It's a perfect opportunity to see things you never had time to see or get involved with interests you never had enough time for when you were working. It's a great time to see more of your family and friends. And you might want to get involved in charity work or volunteering.

Of course, retirement can also mean aches and pains and taking twelve different pills for breakfast as your body gets older. Having adequate medical support and the means to pay for the services you need is key to having a happy retirement.

This may seem a long way away right now. Maybe you're in your twenties, focused on working hard and playing just as hard. But you're going to retire sometime, and how much you're able to enjoy your retirement depends on how much preparation you do right now. It's making an investment in your future self.

Phases of retirement

Most of us think of 'retirement' as a single stage of life. But in fact, there are different phases of retirement. At sixty, you might want to embark on a new artistic or sporting venture, or go around the world; at eighty, you'll probably be rather more sedentary even if you stay in good health.

Acknowledgement phase

I'd argue we need to see retirement as starting as early as your late twenties. You acknowledge that birthdays keep coming and you're not twenty-one anymore. You might not be ready to shift focus completely from career development to planning your retirement, but you should be thinking about how you want to retire and how you want to fund that retirement, in the same way you might want to plan for a family or for starting your own business at some point. Let's call that the acknowledgment phase.

Pre-retirement phase

You'll need to start thinking in a more precise and practical way once you get into your fifties. This is the pre-retirement phase, the last ten years or so before you retire. This is the time you'll get a clearer idea of your total savings and pension entitlements, so you can plug any gaps. You'll want to check the balances in savings plans such as 401k or 457 (if you're in the US), or SIPPs (if you're in the UK), and check your entitlement to basic benefits by checking the retirement estimate calculator in MyCalPERS if you're in California in the US (CalPERS is the largest US public retirement fund with over two million members - other states have similar schemes such as NPERS in Nebraska and MSERS in Massachussetts). If you're in the UK, ask for a pension forecast at www.gov.uk/check-state-pension. Compare your current spending with that income and see how it checks out. If you want to check out what your state pension entitlement is expected to be in the US, you can check this on the SSA's website.

Depending on what you find out in the pre-retirement phase, you might decide to invest more in the next few years. You might look at your other assets and see if you could use them to create additional income. If you have a guest cottage you use when family come to stay, or a spare room, you might consider taking a lodger or doing AirBNB lets, for instance. You might also start thinking about ways to make your money go further, such as downsizing, or even moving to a cheaper area or even country in retirement. You also need to think about any debts you have remaining; this might be a good time to pay your home loan off, if you haven't already.

A session with a financial advisor can really help. They won't be able to change the basic math, but they will be able to suggest the most cost-efficient ways of addressing any shortfall. Be careful to choose a reputable advisor. Anyone telling you about 'alternative' investments (from jatropha plantations to a wine cellar) is unlikely to be on the level. Another good reason to use an advisor is that they should be able to show you all the different choices that you will be able to make at retirement, which can be complex.

At this point, it's worth looking at your investments and seeing whether you want to rebalance your portfolio. If markets crash just before you are due to retire, you have a difficult choice: wait a few years till your pension fund regains its value or retire anyway but on less than you'd hoped. So, if you don't want to take the risk, you might want to shift your portfolio gradually from equities towards less volatile investments like bonds and cash, or to a more conservative equity or fund selection.

Finally, this is a good time to divide your spending into necessities (needs) and discretionary spend (wants). These might vary depending on your circumstances. If you live in the middle of nowhere, a car is a necessity. If you're a New Yorker or a Londoner, maybe it's more of a luxury. It's a good idea to get the necessities covered by a steady, inflation-adjusted income payout, so you know that whatever happens to your other assets and investments, you'll survive.

Early retirement

From sixty-two to seventy, retirement will need a bit of adjusting to. This is the time when you'll be glad to have given some thought earlier on to the question of what you want to do with the rest of your life. You may want to stay in your profession but in a different role, for instance as part of a training business or professional body. You may want to travel, to volunteer for a local charity, or even to change career and take on something entirely new.

When retirement begins, of course, is a complicated question. Some boomers may get an unpleasant surprise when they check the age at which they can claim their pension. In the UK, the retirement age has gone up from sixty-five to sixty-seven, while a lot of women have found their expected retirement age of sixty was first leveled with men's at sixty-five, and then increased to sixty-seven as well. In the US, though you could retire at sixty-two, your benefits would be 72% higher if you waited till you were aged seventy to make your claim.

Some new retirees find they spend more than they expected in the first few years. It's always worth taking another look at your budgets and seeing how they stack up in reality.

There may be a honeymoon phase - traveling, using your leisure time, or just staying in bed past alarm clock time, can be enjoyable. You carry on doing things you were doing, without having to go to work in between.

Disenchantment

After a while, the novelty can wear off. You may feel disappointed. You might wonder how you answer the question: "What do you do?" at parties, feel you're letting time go to waste, or find there's not really enough money to do things you want to do. You may also find that friends you made through work drift away now you're not working.

In that case, you'll need to reorientate yourself to find fulfillment. If you remember having career counseling when you were in your late teens, the process you'll need to go through is similar. It involves evaluating your skills and what's important to you and finding something appropriate. You may want to volunteer; for instance, you could work at a Repair Cafe, helping people fix things, or volunteer to help new arrivals to the country with their English. You might even want to go back to college; retired solicitor Archie White completed his fine arts degree at ninety-six. Or you might help with a sports team, get involved in amateur theater, or even start to compete in veteran sports. My friend's father is working on a project to transcribe medieval French texts such as wills and property deeds via a local university. He's still a youngster though, at eighty-eight.

Mid-retirement

From seventy to eighty may see your expenditure decrease. You might be traveling less, or you might have downsized, or having a slightly less active life. You'll also most likely have settled down to a fairly stable lifestyle, even if you did the round-the-world backpacking thing for a few years. But of course, things don't get any cheaper, which is why it's important to ensure you are protected from the effects of inflation. Fortunately, you'll find CalPERS helps you adjust to the increased cost of living with the annual COLA (Cost Of Living Adjustment) if you live in California in the US (other state pension funds also offer a COLA). In the UK, the state pension is 'triple locked,' being linked to average earnings as well as to inflation, with a 2.5% rise if neither inflation nor earnings have risen that much. However, if you took a simple annuity that isn't index-linked, or if your investments have performed badly, you might find your purchasing power diminishes.

Mid-retirement is a good time to revisit your plans for your estate. It may also be a good idea to give a child or trusted friend a 'power of attorney' so that if anything makes you unable to act on your own behalf, they will be able to carry out your wishes.

Later retirement

From about the age of eighty onwards often involves higher healthcare costs. In the US, Medicare will cover many costs, but you still may need to meet co-payments. In the UK, while most healthcare is free for pensioners, you may need to pay for services such as chiropody or for care support. You might need to get a full-time carer or move into a care home or assisted living facility.

You may well have less energy than you used to. Though some people continue to volunteer, others cut down their activities or take a less active role.

What are the key features of retirement? Some myths demolished

Retirement means no job

This isn't strictly true; you may have finished your previous career, but there's no law against you getting another job. Most retirees develop a new schedule, whether it's volunteering, undertaking church activities, playing regular sports, or getting a new job. Many retirees enjoy a part-time job; others go full-time into contracting or interim management or set up a business of their own.

Retirement means no pay

Again, this isn't strictly true. A lot will depend on how well you've prepared for your retirement. Some people find that they still have bills to pay, even a home loan outstanding, and they may have to give up some of their dreams. On the other hand, many retirees discover that without the cost of the commute, and with the kids now embarked on their own careers, money goes further than it used to.

But be careful! Tempting as it may be to spend all your money in those first few years, you'll want to keep a bit of cash back in case you have medical bills or other emergencies.

Retirement means togetherness

For many couples, that doesn't last long. You used to see each other in the evening after work. Now you're at home all day together, you might discover some sides of your spouse you didn't know and might not much like. That can be particularly the case if one partner has done a lot of thinking about what they want out of retirement, and the other hasn't.

If one of you has been the breadwinner and the other a homebody, you may need to rethink your relationship quite extensively. You don't need to spend every moment of the day together. In fact, it's healthy if you have independent interests. On the other hand, maybe without the stress of busy careers you'll be able to rediscover the reasons you first fell in love.

Retirement means you can travel

But you might actually be traveling less if you had a job with extensive travel requirements. And when you do travel, you might not be staying in five-star hotels; your budget may only manage a motel or a bed and breakfast. You may have had a company car and of course you were meeting people all the time; you may have been doing deals, or speaking at conferences, and getting respect, and now you're just another oldie.

Retirement means poverty

I hope that once you've read this book, you'll be able to make sure that in your case, it's a myth. However, for a lot of people, it isn't. More and more Americans are living paycheck to paycheck, even those getting good salaries. But when they stop working, what will they live off? The horrible truth is that unless you take action now, you're not going to have a wealthy retirement. Finding the money to save for retirement is always difficult, but it could be a choice between pulling your belt in now and misery later.

Some downsides of retirement

There are a few other downsides people won't tell you about, too.

Much as you hated the office Christmas party, the social life of the office, the excitement of working on projects, and the water cooler or coffee break, are all things that some retirees miss.

You may also miss the structure of the working day. True, you never have to catch the commuter train or punch a clock or fill in a timesheet again, but unless you create your own routine, life can feel aimless and unstructured. Retirees who have a regular daily practice such as doing tai chi or yoga first thing, or getting into the garden at lunch time, are generally happier than those who just coast. This has been shown in many studies. One in particular by The University of Pittsburgh found that seniors who consistently get up early and remain active throughout the day are happier and perform better on cognitive tests than those with irregular activity patterns. This research suggests that patterns of activity, not just activity intensity, are vital to both healthy aging and mental health.

Scams are a big downside, and you may not be prepared for that. Scams targeting retirees are on the rise. Scammers think older people will have lost touch with technology and might be swayed by an authoritative voice telling them, "You need to give me your bank password or your credit card will be canceled." They also think older people have plenty of money. The National Council on Aging says there were 92,371 older victims of fraud in 2021 in the US; all together, they lost $1.7 billion – up 74% on the year before. Often, scammers pretend to be from US government agencies such as Medicare, the IRS, or social security, or make a call about an impending lawsuit. There are also computer support scams; Microsoft doesn't normally phone people up demanding money! And you'll need to beware of emails or calls from someone trying to get your grandchildren out of jail or treated after a traffic accident – they're likely to be scams if there's a request for money involved. Once retired, you'll be able to keep yourself up to date on such scams by checking anti-virus sites and consumer organizations. You can also check out https://www.usa.gov/common-scams-frauds or (in the UK) Citizens' Advice.

You also need to think about your health. Even if you've been robustly healthy all your life, as you age, your immune system will become weaker, making it more difficult to fight off colds and flu. If you've had a stressful career with long hours, all that sleep deprivation could catch up with you, too. Fidelity expects Americans retiring in 2022 to spend an average of $315,000 in health and medical expenses! In the UK, you'll be surprised to find how some vital services *aren't* covered by the NHS (though eye tests and prescriptions are free if you're over sixty): chiropody treatment, mobility scooters, wheelchairs, special dietary requirements and vitamin supplements won't be covered (except in certain circumstances, such as foot health checks for those with Type 1 diabetes).

Chapter Two

MISTAKES PEOPLE MAKE AND HOW TO AVOID THEM

In this chapter, I want to look at big mistakes that people make in their retirement planning, and how you can avoid them. Some of them are very easy to make, but on the upside, they're also quite easy to avoid.

Mistakes people make

Having no plan

Having any plan at all, however rough and ready, is better than having none. "I will save 10% of my money" is better than "I'll think about it later." Of course, you'll want to go further if you have any sense. For instance, you'll want to know what returns you're making, and you'll need to think about your target retirement income. If retirement is still a long way off, you may not have a great level of detail, but you can think about 'what if' scenarios: what if your career plateaus by the time you're thirty-five; what if you end up running your own business?

Closer to retirement, you may need a lot more detail, but even so, you might still have two or three different courses of action you could take.

For instance, you could trade down your home to free up capital for your pension fund, or retire later to get a higher income, either of which might deal with a shortfall in funds.

According to PWC, a quarter of American adults have no retirement savings and only just over a third think their retirement planning is on track. It's scary that nearly two-thirds of the US population either don't have a retirement plan or have one they're not sure will give them what they need in retirement. Young people in particular do very poorly – 42% of eighteen- to twenty-one-year-olds have no retirement savings at all. That's robbing them of the chance to use the effect of compounding in their favor.

You will need to take some time and do some tough thinking to make your plan. That said, you don't need to be a rocket scientist, a math whiz, or a finance genius to do it; you just need to think through your needs and your investments in some detail. For instance, think through how you want to live in retirement. If you currently live in a big city and eat out a lot, spend a lot on going to events, and want to continue that lifestyle in retirement, you'll have a different budget in mind from someone who currently has the same lifestyle but who dreams of retiring to an off-grid country cabin or to a low-cost country like Ecuador, Thailand or Portugal.

You may also find it difficult to save enough. That in turn demands more planning. For instance, you could look for hidden savings by canceling subscriptions or refinancing your home loan, transferring the money you save to your retirement account.

Having a plan but not following it

Even for those who have retirement plans, PWC estimates Americans in the cohort approaching retirement (aged fifty-five to sixty-five) have a median of just $120,000 in their plans. That's only enough for $1,500 a month over fifteen years of retirement and doesn't even begin to take account of longer life expectancies and higher healthcare costs. Many of these people's plans should have worked, but they failed to take account of changing conditions, or took 'holidays' from saving and never made up the shortfall.

In the UK, research by Unbiased shows that a fifth of Brits still have no pension savings at all and people nearing retirement aren't much better. At least 17% of people in the UK aged fifty-five and over admit to having no pension savings.

Sometimes things get in the way – it might be medical emergencies, children's college fees, or a period of unemployment. Sometimes saving for retirement takes a back seat to an expensive wedding, honeymoon, vacation or car. And sometimes people just... forget! But it's important, once you have your plan, to keep coming back to it, and making sure you're on track.

Thinking it is too early to plan your retirement

It's weird that a couple of thirty-somethings with a baby will already be planning for the costs of its education but may still feel it's way too early for them to think seriously about retirement. The earlier you think, the longer you can have your money working hard for you.

And of course, you never know what might lie in wait. For instance, you might be fortunate enough to make good money in your twenties and thirties, but then an economic crisis could cost you your job and you could then find it difficult to get a job at the same level as before. If you started early and boosted your retirement savings while you were earning good money, that's one less thing you need to worry about; you can stop saving till you get your finances on the level again. If, on the other hand, you had only just started putting money away for retirement, your plans will be badly derailed.

Even an investment of just $100/£100 a month could make a difference of thousands of dollars/pounds to your future retirement income.

These are planning mistakes. Now we come to execution mistakes – that is, mistakes made in actually carrying out the plan.

Using a savings account for retirement savings

According to Transaminase, two-thirds of workers in the US use a bank account to save for retirement. But that could hurt in the long run.

Although money in the bank is 'safe' compared to stocks or bonds, it can't generate the same long-term returns. While that might not make a big difference over a couple of years, over thirty or forty years' saving for a pension, it means you'd have to put substantially more money in to get the same retirement income (besides, if you have large pensions savings, remember the FDIC in the US only insures you up to $250,000 per bank, per person and per account type. If you're in the UK, banks are authorized by the Prudential Regulation Authority, which is protected by the Financial Services Compensation Scheme (FSCS). This will insure a maximum of £85,000 per person for each 'authorized institution' or banking group).

Money in the bank has another disadvantage, too, compared to other savings methods such as IRAs, ISAs, or 401ks (if you're in the US) or SIPPs (if you're in the UK). It's fully taxable, so not only will you get a low rate of interest, you'll pay tax on it too.

Treading the wrong risk path

There's a golden mean with retirement savings, an ideal balance between extreme risk and extreme safety. You don't want to risk your entire post-retirement lifestyle on a lucky gamble, but you equally don't want a bank account that is totally safe but doesn't pay good returns.

A 2022 report from Fidelity suggested that a quarter of boomers in the US have way too much risk in their portfolios, perhaps simply because they don't actively rebalance them. Good stock market performance over a decade led to them becoming much too highly weighted in equities, particularly for investors who are due to retire within the fairly short term.

How much risk is 'too much' though? Conventional rules of thumb suggested equity investment as a percentage of an investor's portfolio should equate to 100 minus their age. This means 80% equities at twenty, 40% at sixty. However, this rule of thumb was based on lower age expectancies. Perhaps now you should use 110 or even 120 as the basis – so a sixty-year-old should have between 50% and 60% equity.

It's also worth noting that the old rules of thumb applied to a world in which bonds made a real return, which hasn't been the case in the past decade. Ultra-low interest rates account for investors holding more equity risk, since shifting an equity portfolio into bonds would not allow the owner to create a reasonable income.

The key is that you need the right *balance* of risk. For instance, you could hold 90% equities if you wanted, but that should be widely based. A lot of employees own very significant blocks of their own company's stock, but not much else. That exposes them to a much higher level of risk than holding, say, the equivalent amount of an S&P 500 index fund, which would give them broad exposure to the whole US market. The equivalent of the S&P 500 in the UK is the FTSE 100.

And that's another bad investment mistake – not diversifying properly. For instance, real estate has some attractions as a way of investing in predictable, long-term income streams. But holding a single rented apartment as an income source represents a considerable risk: a bad tenant, a poor local economy, or a new residential development three blocks away could all impact your investment.

On the other hand, owning a number of stock market quoted real estate companies (REITs) represents a better diversification of risk while still delivering the same qualities of stable and predictable income. And of course, you also avoid the 'tenants, toilets and trash' aspects of being an actual landlord.

Not dealing with debt

This is a major mistake if you're trying to build your retirement plan. Student loans, housing loans, even business loans can all eat into your available income for savings with their requirement for debt service. If you're living off your credit card, you shouldn't be!

Your income will drop when you stop working. Your retirement income is intended to cover your living costs, not the cost of servicing debt. So you shouldn't look at your retirement plan as something separate from your general budgeting; you'll want to see how you can pay off major debts before you retire, as well as creating a regular income through your investments.

However, if you're close to retirement and you have just a couple of years' home loan left to pay off, it's probably best to concentrate on boosting your retirement income rather than trying to pay off the debt early. So you do need to think about priorities. Using a financial advisor could save you making a mistake here.

Remember to pay off the costliest loans first, that is, the loans with the highest interest. Credit cards and personal loans are usually the most expensive, then car loans, and home loans are usually the cheapest. The more quickly you deal with your debts, the easier it will be to fund your retirement.

A particular difficulty for some retirees is their status as co-signers for student debt for their children or grandchildren. If US federal loans default, social security benefits could be garnished by up to 15% to service the loan. It may be best to ensure these loans are paid down before you retire. Some lenders will also release a co-signer once the main borrower has established a good repayment record.

Not taking advantage of work policies

Many employers can be surprisingly generous when it comes to pensions, and that's why it's almost always a mistake if you are not taking advantage of work policies. If your company is prepared to pay for your pension, this is free money - don't miss out by failing to fill in the forms. You should also take care of whatever schemes are available for healthcare or car leasing; you'll get a better bargain than you would on your own, freeing up money for your investments.

Also make sure that if your company is willing to match your own pension contributions, for instance in a 401k, you contribute enough to take advantage of the offer. Vanguard says that among the plans it offers, the median level of matching is 5% - that means you'd be putting 5% of your salary into a pension, but your employer's matching funds would make it up to 10% of your salary. In the UK, many employers will either match or exceed your own contributions you put into your company pension plan.

Not planning for tax

This is a really major mistake. You really need to understand how your investments are taxed and how your retirement income will be taxed. I'm sorry, but however smart you are, you are not smarter than the tax system (Al Capone wasn't).

Some retirement plans are *tax deferred*. You don't pay tax on returns on your investment, but you'll pay tax when you take your income. Examples are UK salary-based pension schemes and the 457B plan in the US. When you're budgeting for your life as a retiree, you need to think about this income *net*, after you pay tax on it, to see if it will be enough.

In the UK, you'll pay tax on any income over your personal allowance (which is currently £12,570), though you can take a 25% lump sum tax-free from your pension. You then won't pay any tax unless you have actually started taking money out.

In the US, you'll have to pay federal income tax on your pension and on any withdrawals from tax-deferred investments such as IRAs and 401ks. Different states, however, have different rates of tax on pensions; some don't tax pensions. If you move state, even if you earned all your pension in another state, you are only liable for tax in your state of residence.

You should also think about the tax implications of the way you invest. Over time, the tax breaks you get from schemes such as SIPPs (UK) and 401ks (US) can be worth a lot of money. Don't forget that just like your investments, the power of compounding works on the tax you *didn't* have to pay because of the tax break on your pension investment. Holding assets in most pension schemes (and some other types of investment scheme) also means you don't pay tax on dividend income or capital gains while your money is invested. Over the years, particularly once your investment has increased in size, that's quite a saving, and should boost your returns.

Not investing enough in the future

Of course, not investing in the future is a mistake, and it's a very common mistake. It's not easy to visualize the relationship between your savings and an eventual retirement income, and so often people's best guesses about what they need to save turn out very wide of the mark. In the US, the move from traditional employer-provided pensions to 401ks has increased inequalities, with Black, Hispanic, female, lower-income and non-college-educated workers all highly disadvantaged.

Figures from the Economic Policy Institute show that nearly half of American families have no retirement savings at all. There's also increasing polarization between the 'haves' (the top 10% of families have $320,000 retirement savings) and the 'have nots' (the median retirement savings amount is just $7,800).

In the UK, B&CE's financial models show that state and workplace pension saving are unlikely to achieve adequate retirement incomes for the majority of savers. Less than 40% of households are on target to achieve a moderate standard of retirement income; only 4% are on track to be 'comfortable' in retirement.

Very few of those with inadequate pensions are ready to make the lifestyle changes they'd need to deal with lower incomes. In fact, many of them will probably end up continuing to work way past normal retirement age to pay their way.

Basing a pension plan on late retirement

This is a classic mistake. Many people assume they'll 'never retire,' or keep working in the family business till their seventies, so they think they won't need their retirement funds till well after the state pension age. However, that's not a safe assumption to make when you're saving. Retirement can be forced, due to ill health, corporate policies, or government action. The money needed ought to be there, even if it's not called on till later.

When you plan your retirement income, assume you'll retire at standard pension age. Any savings you make or extra returns you gain by retiring later are a bonus but are not to be depended on.

Paying high bills

This can make saving for retirement difficult. It's human nature to want to use a pay rise to afford a higher standard of living but think of putting a third of every pay increase into extra savings rather than extra expenditure.

The snowballing effect can really come into play when you scale up your lifestyle. A larger house means higher energy bills, higher tax bills, more furniture to buy, higher insurance premiums. You may also have moved to a better neighborhood, but many local shops and services cost more than they did where you lived before.

The answer isn't to be ridiculously stingy; simply don't spend every dollar of a pay raise.

Divorce

This is a terrible thing in pensions terms. The more times you divorce and remarry, the more ways the pie is going to have to be split. Divorced men and women generally need a 30% uplift in income to maintain the same standard of living they had before divorce.

Women often suffer the worst. Some lose their homes, many lose their health insurance, one in five falls into poverty, and three-quarters of women with child-support orders don't get all the money they're entitled to. Often, retirement is a long way from a woman's mind in such circumstances. Unfortunately, that, together with lack of funds, means many women approach retirement without nearly enough savings. Men may see their paychecks reduced as the state takes child support out of their gross pay.

It would be easy to say, "Just don't get divorced." But if you do end a marriage, make sure you check in with a financial advisor to see what the potential outcome on your retirement could be.

Skipping the paperwork

This is a big mistake. Lending friends or family money without a signed agreement specifying when it has to be repaid, for instance, often leads to problems further down the road. If you're a partner or founder of a business and you don't have detailed documentation including (among other things) your right to sell, powers of first refusal, and right to use your stake as collateral for a loan, you need to take care to ascertain the status of the asset before you can count on it for retirement. If you're locked into your shares for two years after stopping work, you'll need other income in the meantime. Always make sure deals are properly supported by documentation.

Gambling

This might look out of place here, but it isn't. A small gamble, such as a game of penny-stakes poker between friends, can be fun, but gambling can be insidiously addictive. A proliferation of new casinos, together with highly accessible internet gaming sites, are irresistible to those with unfilled emotional needs, offering excitement, human contact, distraction, and the apparent chance of riches. Sometimes, a gambling habit starts after the death of a partner, as the survivor tries to cope with loneliness and grief.

It's not an answer, and the worst thing is that it can lead to the loss of a lifetime's savings.

If you're not of retirement age yet, of course, gambling could still be an issue. Sometimes, with cryptocurrencies, and with trading sites like Robin Hood, it can be difficult to distinguish investment from gambling. If you're day trading rather than buying shares or funds to hold, are you sure your money wouldn't be better applied to a less glitzy but more long-term investment?

Failing to consider inflation

This is a classic mistake. While you can ignore inflation in the short term, over a number of years it adds up alarmingly. The period since 2007 saw inflation at just 2-3% a year in both the UK and the US. But even at just 2% a year inflation, in terms of purchasing power, $50,000 will only be worth about $30,000 in twenty-five years' time.

Your investments need to create a real return, that is, to rack up a higher return than the inflation rate. Right now, if you left money in the bank at 3% interest, with prices rising by 8% a year, you'd be losing out. That might mean you need to save more than you'd originally thought – which is not great news, but easier to deal with sooner rather than later.

Having a plan is vital. But it's not just a plan you put in place at, say, thirty-two, and keep in place forever. You need to keep actively evaluating your savings and ensuring your retirement goals are still the same and are still being met.

Having a plan set in stone

This is a mistake. Throughout your life you'll change, and you'll change your ideas of what's important and what isn't, what you want to do with your life and what life's too short for. You'll grow older and probably wealthier, so your investments will need to be tracked so that they're still appropriate for where you want to be. Tax write-offs might become more important as you become wealthier, for instance.

If you have the time and expertise to manage your own investments and keep them on track, there's no reason you shouldn't. On the other hand, if you doubt your ability to do this, it's worth having a financial advisor, or using a robo-advisor like Betterment or SoFi (if you're in the US) or Wealthify (if you're in the UK) to ensure your investments are kept up to scratch. Generally, you'll want to reduce the risk of your investments as you grow older, by diversifying (and traditionally by holding fewer equities and more bonds). You'll also want to rebalance at least once a year, cutting investments which have grown too large for your portfolio (for instance if a single stock has grown to 10% of your total).

Keep evaluating your savings. Might you need to retire later, or could you perhaps retire earlier than you'd expected? Might you end up with a lower income than you'd expected? What could you do about that? Do you have other sources of income? If you're asking these questions every year, you're unlikely to end up with any surprises when you want to retire.

Not looking after your health

Finally, a really big retirement mistake is not looking after your health. You will not be happy, no matter how much you save for your retirement, if stress, bad eating, and poor lifestyle choices leave you in pain or unable to enjoy daily life. Remember that retirement is about your health as well as your wealth.

So try to have a balanced lifestyle with regular exercise, healthy eating and a mindfulness practice (such as meditation or yoga). Rather than splashing out on a gym subscription, make small changes to your lifestyle: make time for a walk every morning, or have a full afternoon hiking or biking every weekend.

Remember to get good sleep. When you're in your twenties, pulling an all-nighter is no stress, but it'll catch up with you later.

And remember that healthcare has its costs. Even in the UK, where the National Health Service provides free healthcare, you may have to pay for some types of treatment. In the US, you'll want to ensure you have Medicare and, if possible, a complementary long-term insurance plan.

So, now you're aware of how *not* to plan your retirement, let's get on to learning how to do it properly.

Chapter Three

PLANNING AND BUDGETING YOUR RETIREMENT

There's a lot of advice out there about how much you'll need to retire comfortably – this many thousand dollars a year, this percentage of your salary, such and such an amount invested. There are all kinds of rules of thumb. But in fact, retirement is about you, and you're the only one who can plan it.

A pension firm in the UK prepared two forecasts, one for 'minimum' and one for 'comfortable' retirement. 'Comfortable' included 'one foreign holiday a year.' If you're the kind of person who sees retirement as time to catch up on your traveling (like me), that might be completely inappropriate. You'd probably swap the 'eating out once a week' and two cars included in that lifestyle package for a lot more travel!

So you need to do some thinking about what's important to you and what it costs. You have to be specific. For instance, even if you say "travel is important," what does that mean in specific terms? Are you prepared to backpack or live in a small camper van all summer, do you want to stay in good hotels or have a fully specified RV, or do you want two Caribbean cruises a year?

Loving the theater might translate to a budget for Broadway or West End shows, or it might mean becoming a volunteer for your local theater's box office, or a youth theater company. Most likely it's a mix of both. That's the level of detail you'll need to put into your budgeting to make sure you budget not for some archetypal 'average retiree,' but for *you*.

Budgeting

There are actually two reasons you need to budget in order to create your pension plan. First of all, you need an idea of what you might end up spending (in today's money) when you retire. Secondly, if you're going to be able to save enough money to fund your retirement, budgeting effectively will help you ensure you are in control of your finances.

Budgeting can be simple; it's just working out what you spend in an average month. But many people get overwhelmed when they're asked to do it. Many of us get by every month because we 'sort of' know what we earn and what we spend, and if we end up with a positive balance, we're happy. Moving from that implicit understanding to a formal budget isn't always a comfortable thing to do.

The other factor that budgeting introduces is the idea that your monthly budget is part of a strategic plan, that it has a purpose other than just getting to the end of the month with money still in the bank. For instance, the 50/30/20 rule says you should spend roughly 50% of your net income on necessities (housing, food, insurance); 30% on discretionary spending (vacations, entertainment, sports, interests); and 20% should go into savings and investment. That last 20% is strategic – you might try to make it a higher percentage, particularly if your pension plan currently shows you are short of your targets. Fidelity suggests 50/15/5 - 50% essential expenses, 15% retirement savings, and 5% for cash savings – an emergency fund for those little curveballs that life might throw at you.

One simple way to budget is the 'envelope method.' You take your salary in cash, you put the cash in separate envelopes for different purposes. There might be a 'groceries' envelope, 'debt pay-down' envelope, 'kids' envelope, or whichever categories you need. If you're a freelancer, you might have a 'training, education, and networking' envelope. You can spend what's in the envelope, and that's it.

Well, that's the way Nana did it. It's not so simple when you have bank transfers, debit cards, and so on. But there are plenty of apps that can help you use a similar method, such as Goodbudget, EveryDollar, PocketGuard and Fudget. You can also use Mint's budgeting features (Mint is a budgeting and expense-manager app that allows you to easily see your monthly bills, set goals, and build stronger financial habits). You're thinking the same way, but you don't need to carry cash around.

Some banks, like Bank of America, Chase, and UK bank Monzo, will also let you do this.

Remember that your cash savings need to be readily accessible. They're for emergencies like car repairs, temporary unemployment, replacing a broken fridge or washing machine, dropping everything to look after an older relative who's had an accident, or replacing your youngest's mobile (again). So you won't get a good rate of return on that account. Keep an eye on it, as beyond a certain amount (say, six month's salary), you're better off transferring that money into investments that can create a better return. 'Skimming' the fund from time to time can boost your investments while leaving you the security of a cash buffer.

How to budget

Just to get a quick idea of the sorts of numbers that might be involved, it can be good to look at a basic pensions calculator, like https://www.moneyhelper.org.uk/en/pensions-and-retirement/pensions-basics/pension-calculator?source=mas# (if you're in the UK), or https://www.nerdwallet.com/investing/retirement-calculator (if you're in the US). These use some basic formulas to estimate what you need to save, based on your age, salary, savings, and other data that you can input. Generally, they estimate you'll want your retirement income to equate to about 70% of your salary.

When budgeting, you will need to think about:

- Your needs when you reach retirement.
- What you can afford to save right now.
- How many years you have left to save.
- When you will have paid off your home loan.
- How the benefits system may change.
- Any gap between state pension age and the age you want to retire.
- Inflation.
- Taxes on retirement income.
- Healthcare costs.

It's obviously difficult, if you're in your late twenties, to think in detailed terms about what you'll need when you're sixty-five. Your entire life may have changed. You may be living in a different country, have married, divorced or remarried; you might have changed career. So you can use 70-80% of your final salary as a rule of thumb.

(By the way, 'final salary' comes from the days when career progression meant you would be earning your highest salary the day before you retired. This probably doesn't hold for many people these days, particularly those who change career, downshift in their fifties, go back to college or decide to start their own business. But working on new formulas to take increasingly complex working lives into account is something the professionals need to get to grips with).

Start by making a list of your anticipated costs. If you own your home, and you will have paid off your loan, then that will no longer be a cost, but you will still have property taxes, insurance, and utilities. If you spend more time at home than you did while you were working, some of those costs (like heating) might go up; though you can deduct any commuter travel from your budget.

Think about your general costs, such as groceries, which probably won't change very much (apart from an inflation rise); TV, internet, and phone costs; and any services such as cleaning or gardening that you pay for. You can then add pets, clothes, hairdressing and personal treatments, sports or gym memberships, books, music, and so on. Finally, add the costs of your car(s), holidays, and any healthcare plans, life assurance, and charitable donations.

Remember that you may spend more on hobbies and interests once you have more time available. Some people decide to turn hobbies like wood turning, art or furniture restoration into small businesses, adding another source of income in retirement. You may also have a number of one-off expenses from time to time, such as buying a new car, contributing to a grandchild's education or a child's wedding, or home repairs.

You also need to think about where you want to live in retirement. Your existing home may not be where you want to be permanently. You might trade a city apartment for a country smallholding, or a suburban family home for a flat. If you no longer have to work in a particular place, you are free to relocate, and you can factor that into your calculations as a capital input.

As a very rough guide, the US Bureau of Labor Statistics reckons that households in the US run by someone aged sixty-five or over, spend on average $50,220 a year, or $4,185 a month. Of course, a good number of those will be two-person (or more) households, and it's part of the definition of an average that a good number of values fall *below* the average. Trawl around the internet and you'll find other data. For instance, Numbeo is an interesting site that gives the cost of living in different cities across the world, if you're considering moving.

You are not average! But these averages give you some data against which you can plot your own needs. For instance, if you know that you have quite an expensive lifestyle, but your budget gave you a much smaller annual amount, then you know you have forgotten something!

Where will your money come from after retirement?

This used to be the easy question, and answers might be 'the state pension,' or 'my works pension,' or 'my stock portfolio.' Nowadays, it's more complex, and retirement income is likely to come from a number of sources, not always at the same time. For instance, you might decide to retire early from your main employment and run a small business doing leather crafting or consulting. At the same time you could be taking income from your stock portfolio and a small amount from your 401k or company pension. Later on, your social security/state pension will also kick in. You might also have passive income from assets such as rental properties to add to the mix.

In fact, it's always a good idea to have multiple income sources. They may be of different risk types: an annuity-based pension, or the state pension, are virtually riskless, while dividend stocks represent a higher risk but will deliver increasing returns over the long term.

You may also take an income by selling down part of your capital. However, while this is a viable component of retirement income, you need to ensure that you don't take too much early on. It's most useful as a way of evening out 'lumpy' income. For instance, if in one year your rental property needs refurbishing, so your property income is less than half what it should be, selling some stock could fill the gap.

Right now, you should calculate what your retirement income will look like, based on your entitlements to different pension plans, your investment properties and savings, and future savings. You then need to keep assessing whether you're on track. Revisit your budget every so often to make sure it's still realistic and assess your investments to see if they are giving you good enough returns.

Automate everything you can. If you automate contributions to retirement plans and other investments, that money will go straight there, so you won't see it as 'available' and start to spend it as part of your regular income. Running a 'sweep' of your current account at the end of the month and clearing all the money above a certain amount into your investment fund can help boost your savings. You can also boost your savings by reinvesting any dividends paid on your stock trading account on a regular basis, instead of letting cash pile up.

Things to think about

Now you've got some ideas on what you might need in retirement and how your investments to date add up. The gap between the two is what you need to fill. For instance, if you're lucky enough to have rental apartments that produce $30,000 a year net income (and no loans left to pay off), and you want a $50,000 retirement income, then you only have $20,000 of income to find.

Pensions calculators will tell you how much you need to invest to get a certain income. Or you could take a different approach and look at what stock market investments would get you there. The S&P 500 currently yields just under 2%, so to get $20,000 a year you'd need to invest $1,000,000 (20,000 / 0.02). On the other hand, if you were to invest in high-yield stocks you could get 4.3%, which would more than halve the amount you need to $465,116. The FTSE 100 yielded an average of 3.72% in 2022, so to get £20,000 a year, you'd need to invest £537,634 (20,000 / 0.0372).

That calculation, by the way, does not assume that you will sell down any capital; it is based purely on the current income from the stocks. In fact, you *could* retire on less if you were willing to release capital.

But a plan is not all you need. For instance, you'll need the discipline to save something every month. Saving is not 'what's left over;' it's an amount you need to specify and aim to achieve, however hard. Even if your saving is a relatively small amount right now, because of other priorities, try to make a regular input. It's a good habit to build.

You might compare fitness. Being fit isn't something you do after you've fitted everything else into the day, if you have any time left. It's something you spend a certain amount of time on regularly, in order for it to have the right impact on your life. Even if you can only manage a brisk walk a couple of times a week, it's important to make a regular date; you can't leave it all till the summer vacation and say "I'll get fit when I have the spare time!"

Don't see savings as a negation. Yes, there may be some unpleasant choices – give up buying those cappuccinos, live in a less desirable neighborhood or a smaller house than you could afford, or only allow yourself a certain number of clothes purchases a year. But saving is about putting money away for *future* spending. It's about creating a revenue stream for the future and giving yourself financial power. Think about these positive aspects of saving.

In fact, many well-paid professionals find it hard to save, because they think about their money as available to spend, rather than being sufficiently pragmatic to see that it's available to invest, and make *more* money, giving them more independence. Have a read of James Clear's 'Atomic Habits' – he talks about the power of making small changes in your life; it's a very useful and powerful book.

One thing that can help is to get genuinely excited about your investments. That may be one reason direct real estate investment remains so popular: it's easy to get excited about buying an apartment! A friend spends one evening every month selecting stock purchases using Morningstar, with a glass of craft beer in hand. She regards this as top retail therapy.

Remember you'll want to review how you're doing on budgeting. A monthly review is a great idea. You don't need to go into great depth, as all you're looking to do is to see if you're staying on track, and what areas are taking up more or less money than expected. If you find that you can increase your savings quota, why not ratchet it up? There are loads of free resources out there to help with budgeting, or you can use a spreadsheet or pen and paper if you feel happier doing things that way.

If you're married or partnered, make sure that you both understand where you're at in terms of the monthly budget, short-term savings and long-term investments. One of you may be more interested than the other, but you should both understand and agree the budget. Oddly, though boomer women wrestled responsibility for their own financial affairs from men, millennial women seem happier to give it up. But it's not something you can delegate. Many women only find out what a mistake it was to hand all the responsibility to their husbands when they get divorced, it's sad to say.

Prioritizing your financial goals

Of course, retirement is not your only financial goal. You'll have others, such as home ownership, funding life experiences such as sabbaticals, and maybe having children (each child comes with average cost $310,000 or so from age zero to eighteen in the US, or £185,000 if you're in the UK). So you need to prioritize your goals.

For instance, if you have debt, getting out of debt is probably one of the first things you want to do (apart from home loans, which are relatively cheap and long-term). However, you should still try to make some small payments towards a retirement plan. Remember that the effect of compounding makes early investments punch above their weight in terms of long-term return.

Think about what you value in your lifestyle. Children? Friends? Your work? Owning your own place? Having interesting experiences? For instance, a friend decided a corporate career was not for him. He's worked in South Korea, Japan, France, the Gulf and Brazil as an English teacher, which has let him see the world at low cost, while putting aside a good half of his salary as savings and investments. But though he says he can feel at home anywhere in the world, he has never actually owned his home.

Another friend took a very different decision, deciding to buy her own place as soon as she could while she concentrated on her high-flying career in financial software; she hasn't had a vacation in years. You may be less extreme in your preferences, but it's worth sitting down and thinking about what is really meaningful for you.

Feel free to take courageous decisions. If what's really important to you is getting financial independence as soon as possible, don't let yourself drift into a 'keeping up with the Joneses' existence. Just because everyone you work with has a certain lifestyle, that doesn't mean you have to buy in. There may be a number of trade-offs you could make that would really help you get ahead, and some hacks that might help:

- Subsidize home ownership and create an investment asset at the same time by buying a duplex and renting the other half of it out.
- Use AirBNB or house swaps to help fund your vacations (watch out for any permissions you need and be sure to check with your insurer).
- Start a side hustle that can create 'long-tail' income, such as offering training courses or making 'how to' videos.
- Live up to your *last but one* pay raise – don't ratchet up your lifestyle every time your salary goes up.
- Increase your savings percentage every time you are able to.
- If you have paid off a debt, such as a car loan, switch the monthly amount, but pay it to a savings or investment account instead.

In the early years, try to put as much as you can into investing for retirement, whether that's in a regular pension plan or another investment vehicle. Prioritize tax-exempt methods of investing to maximize the effect of compounding. $1,000 or £1,000 invested when you're twenty is worth more than twice as much to your retirement income as $1,000 or £1,000 invested when you're forty.

In fact, it may be easier to save when you're younger. If you're concentrated on getting ahead in your career, and you don't yet have children, you may be able to put a significant amount away. Of course, if you live in an expensive area like Silicon Valley or central London, things could be more difficult.

Make sure that you take the right amount of risk to get good returns. Find out about the stock market. You may decide you want to be an active investor or just to buy more shares in the same four or five Exchange Traded Funds every month to give you exposure to different markets. And then just leave your investments alone. Never mind what the market is doing – it's always going up and down, but you have forty years or more that you can remain invested, with that money working for you. Selecting stocks with a growth bias, and investing in emerging markets, are right for this stage of investment.

As you get into your forties, you'll have a better idea of what kind of retirement you want. You might be tempted to move into lower-risk investments, but you still have twenty years to retirement! So keep the right level of risk assets and stay invested. If you are following the usual career trajectory, you'll be earning well, so the tax breaks you can get by investing in pensions will be useful.

Make sure that during your forties and fifties you keep track of exactly what investments and pension entitlements you have. If the government raises the pension age, for instance, you need to know that, and you might need to save extra funds for supporting retirement before that age. Also, remember to check your statement of wishes – if you don't want your pension going to your ex, for instance!

Chapter Four
SAVINGS AND INVESTMENTS

I'm not a financial advisor, and this book won't give you financial advice. If you want that, I'd recommend finding a good advisor. But what I can do is to explain all the options that are available to you, so that you fully understand the topic and can ask relevant questions and make informed decisions. Most financial advisors have a number of default solutions which aren't bad, but they might not take into account your own preferences, circumstances or wishes.

Some of the issues you'll want to think about as you read this chapter are about your own attitude to risk. For instance, you may not have a great appetite for risk, but you need to ensure you take enough risk to generate investment returns in the long term. Striking the right balance between risk and reward is vital. So you need to understand your own risk tolerance, but also to think about what is the ideal risk for someone in your position. The two may not be the same, so you'll need to do some thinking about how to square this particular circle.

Understanding your risk profile is key to selecting the right investments. You'll want to understand what you're investing in, at least in general terms. The 'black box' investment is almost always a fraud (Bernie Madoff, for instance, said he had a 'secret' trading technique that generated extremely high profits; of course, it didn't exist). You might have different approaches to risk in the long term or medium term from when you are dealing with short-term savings.

Investments can include currencies, bonds, equities (stock or shares), crowdfunding, or real estate. You may hold them directly or indirectly. For instance, you could hold a REIT as an indirect way of holding real estate, or an exchange traded fund (ETF) as an indirect way of holding stocks. These different *asset classes* behave differently. For instance, equities tend to be more volatile than bonds; investment-grade bonds are less volatile than 'junk bonds' (below investment grade, that is, assessed by a credit rating agency as higher risk).

It is always a good idea to spread your risk over different asset classes. That way, if one type of asset underperforms, you have other asset classes which will still generate a positive return.

Always know the tax treatment of any investment you make. Everyone needs to pay tax, but there are legal ways of saving tax on long-term investments. Most pension schemes give a tax break – basically a bribe offered by the government to get people to save!

Social security

The federal government in the US runs the social security program, using taxes paid into a trust fund to pay benefits to those who are eligible. While you're working, you'll pay through payroll taxes, automatically. You can start to take your retirement benefits at any age from sixty-two to seventy. The longer you defer taking your benefits, the more you'll get (social security also offers disability and some other benefits).

Social security will only deliver $20,000 a year on average. That's quite difficult to live on!

The UK equivalent is the National Insurance scheme run by HMRC. Again, contributions are taken out of payroll (or paid directly if you're self-employed); and again, the amount paid is quite small, just £9,630 a year at present if you have full entitlement. Some people lose out because they don't have enough contributions, such as women who have taken a break to look after children, or people who have worked part time or on very low wages.

If social security forms your entire retirement income, you probably won't have to pay tax. However, if you have other income from investments or from employment, you may end up paying tax on your social security income too.

Retirement plans

Many companies offer retirement plans. In the UK, it's now compulsory for employers to offer a basic plan to all workers over twenty-two years old who earn more than £10,000 a year. The minimum contribution is 5% from the employee and 3% from the employer, and employees are automatically enrolled (though they can opt out). In the US, offering a retirement plan isn't obligatory, but many employers do: Coca-Cola, Amgen, Boeing, and Citigroup, for instance. Other employers offer to match employees' contributions to a 401k scheme, which basically doubles your investment.

So before you go any further, you should find out what your company offers. You also might want to find out if the plan offered will cover a surviving spouse or dependent children.

There are two kinds of retirement plans:

1. Defined benefit.
2. Defined contribution.

'Defined benefit' is what you might call an 'old style' pension plan, where you know exactly what you'll get when you retire. That might be stated in absolute terms, as dollars a month, or it might be calculated through a formula considering factors such as your salary and length of service. Such plans are protected (though not 100%) by federal insurance. Most large British companies ran such schemes, but most are now moving towards defined contribution schemes. However, if you work in the public sector. you may still be enrolled in a defined benefit scheme.

'Defined contribution' means that while what you will pay in is a set rate, such as 5% of your earnings, what you get out will depend on investment performance. A 401k is a defined contribution plan, for instance. The contributions may be invested on your behalf or you may be able to control the investments directly. When you retire, you will be able to access the funds in that account.

Because the funds from a defined contribution plan are often used at least partly to purchase an annuity, which will pay a regular income, these are sometimes referred to as 'money purchase' schemes.

In the UK, if you pay into a pension scheme via your employer, you may get *relief at source*. This means that your employer will only take the *net* pension contribution from your salary before paying you. For example, if your tax rate is 20%, and you make £100 contribution, your employer will only subtract £80 from your pay to put into your pension. Your pension provider will then ask HMRC to make up the remaining £20. But most employer-provided pension schemes in the UK now offer a salary sacrifice pension scheme, where you agree to a reduction in your salary in exchange for a pension contribution made by your employer. You therefore save tax and National Insurance on the amount of salary you have sacrificed.

You should also understand the difference between 'tax deferred' and 'tax exempt.' Both offer you a tax advantage, but the difference lies in when you receive the benefit.

- Tax-deferred accounts give you a tax break when you contribute to them (though there are annual limits on what you can contribute). However, you'll pay income tax on money you take out after retirement. Regular IRAs and 401k plans in the US, and SIPPs in the UK, are tax deferred.
- Tax-exempt accounts like the ISA in the UK (not, of course, a pension scheme) and the Roth IRA in the US provide the benefit

when you take money out. The money that you put in comes from your after-tax income, but you pay no tax on the investments you hold or the money you take out.

You might think that just putting off the payment of tax is not a worthwhile benefit. However, tax-deferred schemes work in your favor., since normally your retirement income is lower than your regular income, so you will probably pay a lower marginal rate of tax. Also, you won't be paying income tax on interest and dividends, or capital gains tax on any gains, so your investments will be sheltered from tax while they are growing. That has quite a large impact on your returns over the long term.

Tax-deferred retirement plans

US

The most common tax-deferred plans in the US are the 401k and the traditional IRA. When you pay into such a scheme, you can deduct the amount you contributed from your taxable income. So for instance, if you earned $100,000 and put $20,000 in a 401k, you would only be taxed on income of $80,000.

In 2023, the annual limits for contributions are $22,500 for a 401k, plus $7,500 more if you're over fifty. A further $6,500 can be put into a traditional IRA (plus $1,000 for over-fifties).

Another US defined contribution plan is the simplified employee pension (SEP). This is a grouping of traditional IRAs for a single employer, and unlike traditional IRAs, it allows the employer as well as the individual to make contributions (up to a limit per individual of $61,000 or 25% of employee total compensation). A profit-sharing or stock bonus plan may also be offered to employees.

A major benefit of 401ks is that employers will often match contributions, at a rate of fifty cents to a dollar for every dollar you invest, up to a given percentage of salary.

Employees of some public schools and tax-exempt organizations may be entitled to open a 403b plan (tax-sheltered annuity plan). Here, again, the employer may match contributions. The way the 403b works, including the limits on contributions, is the same as for the 401k.

Tax-deferred plans are good for high earners, because they can reduce taxable income significantly. If you can manage to drop a tax bracket, you'll be taxed on less income *and* at a lower rate – a double whammy! (Note, though, that there is a minimum annual withdrawal when you hit seventy-two; this will be calculated for you by the IRS).

UK

In the UK, you are able to contribute up to £60,000 a year into a pension and get tax relief on this amount. This includes both employee and employer contributions, but you may lose entitlement to some of this if you are a high earner and it can reduce to a minimum of £10,000. You can contribute more, but you won't get tax relief on the excess, but instead will have a tax charge at your marginal rate. If you did not contribute in previous years, you may be able to carry forward that entitlement, to invest more in a tax year when, for instance, you may have received a good bonus. Until recently, there was a lifetime allowance of £1,073,100 for the total value of all your pensions; above this limit, penal tax rates applied. The government recently scrapped this lifetime allowance. You can set up a SIPP (self-invested personal pension) in addition to any employer pension plan you have. These are particularly useful if you're self-employed or if you change jobs frequently.

UK workplace schemes are also tax-deferred schemes. They may include salary sacrifice, in which case they're sometimes known as SMART schemes. You give up part of your salary to make an extra contribution, which your employer will put directly into the pension fund (this is great news for undisciplined savers, since you never get to see the money before it goes into the pension pot!). This can save you and your employer tax and National Insurance contributions.

Employers must enroll you automatically if you are eligible. Even if you are not eligible for auto-enrollment, they must still allow you to join the scheme on request, although if you earn less than £520 a month, they don't have to contribute.

Tax-exempt retirement plans

US

The Roth IRA and Roth 401k are popular tax-exempt accounts. The contribution limits are the same as for traditional IRAs and 401ks, but you don't get tax relief when paying into your pension like you do with a tax-deferred scheme (which in turn means you aren't taxed when withdrawing money). A major advantage of these accounts is that you can access your money in retirement without being pushed into a higher tax bracket. These are great plans if you're just starting your career, with a modest salary. First of all, the tax break on the tax-deferred plan might not be worth much to you right now. Secondly, if you move up the corporate ladder, by the time you retire you might be in a higher tax bracket, so the tax break will be worth more by then.

You can subscribe to both a traditional IRA and a Roth IRA, but the $6,500 limit applies to both combined. You should note that unlike traditional accounts, Roth accounts cannot receive a matching contribution from your employer.

You can start to withdraw funds tax free once you are fifty-nine. If you need access to funds before that date, you'll have to pay a 10% penalty.

UK

In the UK, an ISA (individual savings account) allows you to save £20,000 a year out of your taxed income, and investments held within that wrapper are tax-exempt. You can take money out *whenever you like*, without paying any tax on it. While ISAs are not intended primarily as retirement schemes, they are excellent long-term savings vehicles and very easy to set up. Having tax-free income in retirement may let you pay a lower rate of tax on your pensions.

Converting to a Roth IRA

If you're in the US, you can transfer assets from a traditional IRA, including a 401(k), SEP, or simple IRA, into a Roth IRA. You'll then be able to benefit from tax-exempt payments out of the fund when you retire. This is useful if you won't need the assets for at least five years, expect to be in the same tax bracket when you retire and might not need the funds for your retirement, but want to be able to pass them on as part of your estate.

You will, however, have to pay a penalty to do this, paying back any tax breaks. That will be included in your income for the year, and that could push you into a higher tax bracket (if you're taking a sabbatical, that would be a great time to think about converting!).

And you should note that once you've converted, you cannot convert back again. You have to convert within the tax year that you want the conversion to apply to (i.e., by December 31st), and my advice would be to talk it through with your accountant and/or your financial advisor first.

Now we've had a look at the kinds of schemes you might use to invest, let's look at the types of asset that you can invest in.

Equity investment – stocks

When you invest in stocks, you are investing in business. For instance, if you buy shares in Coca-Cola, you are investing in a tiny percentage of fizzy drink sales all over the world and the profit that Coca-Cola makes from it. You will get two kinds of return. The first is capital appreciation – if the company grows, the stock price should increase – and the second is dividend income (though not all companies pay a dividend).

Stocks can be quite volatile; that is, their prices can go up and down significantly. However, if you look at the underlying business you are buying, it can be quite stable. That's why you need to commit to at least a medium-term investment of five years or so. That's great for a pension fund, but don't put the money you need for next month's groceries into stocks.

You also need to diversify. Just holding Coca-Cola shares is a risky bet; one bad quarter could leave your portfolio looking very poorly. On the other hand, if you hold equal amounts of Coca-Cola, Microsoft, Pfizer, JPMorgan Chase, and Exxon Mobil, you have a broader base, not just of individual companies, but of different sectors of the economy. This can be hard to do when you're getting started, though using a low- or no-commission broker can let you buy small amounts of stock. Some, like Robinhood, will even let you buy fractions of stock, if the stock price is very high.

If you want to invest directly, then you'll either need to do your own research or to find an advisor who can help. You'll also need to spend some time and effort on learning about stocks and keeping up to speed.

An employee share ownership plan (ESOP) is a special kind of retirement plan in which an employer contributes its own shares to the pension plan. It's *not* the same as a stock option plan, which gives employees the right to buy shares at a set price after a certain period of time. Be careful if you have one of these – it means your retirement is very heavily dependent on your employer's performance and the performance of its share price.

In the UK, you can invest in a stocks and shares ISA. With its generous £20,000-a-year limit on contributions, it's a great way to save. Many brokers offer inexpensive ISA plans in which you can invest both directly in shares and in unit trusts and other funds.

Dividend investing

This might form part of your retirement savings, but it can also give you a great supplementary income while you're working. Many (though not all) profitable companies pay dividends to their shareholders, distributing part of their profits. American companies pay quarterly, while most UK companies pay two dividends a year, and some European companies only pay once a year. So if you invest in dividend-paying shares, you'll be able to build up a good income stream eventually. You can either reinvest this income to supercharge your returns through the effect of compounding, or use it for a few luxuries in your life, and eventually, as a source of retirement income.

You'll need to get on top of a few numbers. The first is *dividend yield*, which measures the dividend income as a percentage of what you paid for the shares. You can compare this with an interest rate; the two figures deliver the same information. However, with a dividend, you're hoping it will grow in time, which isn't the case with interest.

Some companies don't pay a dividend at all; they reinvest in their own operations. That's true for many tech companies. Some companies are mainly bought by investors who want to see earnings growth, and their dividends might only give a low yield like 1%. Other companies pay higher yields, such as REITs, and firms like Abbvie, Philip Morris and Verizon yield from 3% up to 7%.

The best way to find dividend stocks is to run a stock screener. For instance, on Morningstar, you can use the dividend yield as a search criterion. You can find stocks that apparently pay huge yields, like 11%, but be wary. In many cases, they're high risk, with a lot of debts and not much profit. That's where another number comes in – dividend cover. If the company doesn't have enough earnings to pay the dividend, it's a bad investment. Cover is simply the percentage of earnings that the company pay out. Anything less than 30% is super safe, up to 60% is pretty normal, and you ought to start worrying at 80%, *except for REITs,* which are a different kind of animal).

There are three different schools of dividend investing:

- **High-yield investing** – getting the maximum yield, for instance, if you want retirement income.
- **Dividend-growth investing** – investing in a company which may not pay the highest yield, but which are growing their dividends (e.g., Microsoft).
- **A balance of yield and growth**.

Dividend-growth investing will bring great returns if you get started early on, but you have to be patient for it to work. If you're older and looking primarily for a source of complementary income, you might want to shift towards more of a high-yield strategy.

Bonds – fixed income

Another asset class you can invest in is fixed income – bonds, treasury bills or notes. All of these are a form of IOU, issued by a government, company, or other organization, which entitle the holder to repayment on a certain date and a given rate of interest in the meantime. Unlike shares, they do not give you any participation in the business, and the 'coupon' (interest payment) will not rise, unlike a dividend. So, they don't have the growth characteristics of equity.

On the other hand, bonds have a certain safety built in. They give bondholders the right to be paid out on any liquidation ahead of shareholders. And while a company can decide whether or not to pay a dividend, it is obliged to pay the coupon on its bonds. The risk of default on, say, US or UK government bonds, is next to nothing, though some corporate or emerging-market government bonds are higher risk.

Bonds come in different maturities. For instance, US treasury notes are issued with ten years to run, while US treasury bonds run for twenty to thirty years. This gives bonds stable, long-term income characteristics which are highly suited to pension funds.

However, bonds are traded, just like shares, and their prices can go up and down depending on the market's view of the risk involved and on prevailing interest rates.

Real estate

Real estate is a third major asset class, and we'll talk about it in more detail later when talking about passive income. It's an investment that tends to grow with inflation, as house prices rise. It also generates a long-term, stable income stream in the form of rent.

Some people will want to buy a rental property or buy a property to renovate and then sell. Renovating can be good if you're keen on DIY, but be careful that you have a good, up-to-date knowledge of exactly what buyers are looking for in your area. If you're not good at DIY, another great option is to use professional tradespeople to do the work for you!

REITs

If you're useless at DIY and you don't have enough money to buy a property directly, you can invest indirectly via real estate investment trusts (REITs) or through shares in property investment groups. REITs pool investors' money and are able to buy office buildings, malls, logistics centers, and even cellphone towers and farmland; they then manage the property and pay a dividend to investors out of the rental income. Some experts believe you should put as much as 30% of your portfolio into REITs.

Crowdfunding

Another way of investing in real estate is crowdfunding, whether through ownership or (more often) by helping to debt finance a development. Where the loan notes are backed by the security of the asset, and the developer has a good track record, this can be a good way to increase your returns, but ensure you use a reputable crowdfunding platform.

House flipping

For those with a little more funds available, or who are able to borrow, house flipping can work nicely.

House flipping can be a side hustle or a business, depending on how you structure it. Many people get started buying a house that needs relatively light refurbishment as their first home, doing it up while they're living there and selling it at a profit. Since you'll likely be able to get a home loan, this is relatively low risk, and the profit is partly or fully tax exempt unless the tax inspector thinks you're doing this for a business (if you live somewhere for two or three years and sell it, you're fine; if you move home every six months, you may end up paying tax).

However, if you want to do this as a business, you'll need to have a business plan and you'll need to have both property prices for the area and refurbishment costs at your fingertips. For flipping as a business, you'll need commercial funding, which will cost more than a home loan, and you need to be able to complete and sell the property within the loan term, or interest costs will eat into your profit margin. Don't forget that as well as interest, you'll have insurance, utilities and tax costs that increase with every day you have to hold the property.

It's a big effort, unless you have a background in the building trade. Most business flippers build up a team of regular contractors they know they can depend on. And it's also a risk, as one bad deal could theoretically wipe out your profits from two or three good ones. The better you know your local market, the better you will do. Share your numbers with your tradespeople. A friend has a roofer and a general contractor who visit houses with her. Between the two of them, they give a pretty good estimate of the costs, and they also have a canny idea of what houses really sell for, which is sometimes quite different from what a real estate agent will tell you.

You can limit your risk by not paying too much. Make sure you know what the upgrades will cost and what the property will be worth once renovated. The 70% rule is a good rule of thumb: don't pay more than 70% of the after-repair value *less* repairs needed. Also, make sure you don't underestimate the work involved. This is a hard work side hustle, not a way to get rich quick.

US readers, did you know you may be able to use your retirement funds to do a professional house flip? Do it with a 401k and all your profit is tax-deferred!

Not all real estate investments share the same risk profile. For instance, buying an apartment in the third phase of a resort that has already become established is lower risk than buying an apartment in a completely new resort. Buying shares in a company that rents out properties is lower risk than buying shares in a developer, which relies on selling properties for its income. Ensure that if you invest in real estate, you take only the appropriate level of risk.

Index funds, ETFs, and mutual funds

Technically speaking, these are not another asset class, but another way of investing in different asset classes. You can invest in a bond fund, an equity fund, a real estate fund, or even in different metals, agricultural commodities, or currencies through funds.

Index and mutual funds and ETFs are all collective investments which pool many individual investors' money. However, the way they operate is quite different.

- **Actively managed** mutual funds try to beat the market. They may have highly paid fund managers, do a lot of analysis, and take contrarian positions against the market. The downsides are that some of them miss their targets and they're a costly way to invest.
- **Passively managed** mutual funds and **exchange traded funds** (ETFs) try to copy the market, instead of trying to beat it. That means you should get pretty much the average market performance, and it substantially reduces the cost of investment.
    - Mutual funds often invest in index funds and they generally have charges lower than actively managed funds. They're bought either from the fund manager or via an online platform.
    - ETFs are slightly different in that they are traded like ordinary stock, on the stock market. They generally charge even lower fees than other index funds. ETFs often charge fees of 0.1% to 0.4% of the fund value per year, while some actively managed mutual funds charge as much as 1.5% plus performance fees.

Though the press often likes to report mutual funds and ETFs as an 'either/or' story, you can use both to invest. For instance, you could use ETFs as your base for a portfolio, buying US big-cap, US smaller-cap, European and Asian ETFs. Then you could add a couple of specialized funds to add areas like biotechnology or private equity. By using ETFs, you get a wide exposure to the equity market at extremely low cost.

The best-known mutual funds are equity based, but you will also find bond funds, 'balanced' funds which use both, money market funds (investing in short-term instruments to make a better return than a bank account), income funds (which invest in equities that pay dividends), and specialty funds investing in different countries or sectors.

Another advantage of ETFs is that they are exchange traded – that is, you can buy them just as easily as you could buy a share, through any online broker. You can buy them in small quantities, too, whereas some mutual funds have a high entry point, with a minimum investment of $5,000 or even $10,000 required.

Remember to check that a fund 'does what it says on the tin.' Always look through to the portfolio holdings and make sure you're not duplicating your investments. For instance, if you bought an S&P 500 ETF and then bought Amazon shares, you'd actually be doubling up on Amazon, which is one of the ETF's biggest holdings. Morningstar is a very useful tool, but some brokers also have great tools for portfolio analysis.

Whatever mix of ETFs and mutual funds you pick, you'll be able to achieve effective diversification with a much smaller amount of money than if you bought individual stocks, reducing the overall risk of your retirement portfolio.

There are different types of fund available, so let's take a look at them.

Funds

- **Stock funds** invest in shares. They may be generalist, or targeted towards a particular sector (e.g., healthcare funds), or a particular geography (e.g., emerging market funds) or size of company (e.g., small cap funds). Some target capital appreciation, while others focus on generating income.

- **Bond funds** invest in government or corporate bonds. Again, they may have different emphases. Some may try to achieve superior returns by focusing on 'junk bonds' with room for capital appreciation, others may attempt to deliver income while preserving capital by focusing on short to medium-duration, high-quality bonds. Ensure you understand the fund's priorities before you invest.
- While most funds attempt to beat the market, **index funds** aim to replicate the market return. You can get mutual funds which do this, but the best way to invest in indices is through ETFs, which have much lower fees.
- **Balanced funds** invest in both bonds and stocks to create a balanced portfolio that will pay current income as well as maintaining and growing your capital. They are more useful for older investors approaching retirement, or after retirement; younger investors will not get an adequate return from them.
- **Money market funds** invest in very short-dated government bonds and are as safe as you can get from the point of view of capital appreciation. However, they will not pay good returns, so don't even think of investing *except* if you have a very short time till retirement and want to ensure your portfolio value doesn't slump if the market goes down.
- **Hedge funds** use complex trading techniques and often take large bets on equities, currencies, bonds and commodities to attempt to produce high absolute returns. Watch out: they also charge higher fees.
- **Target date funds** invest in a bond/equity mix that is designed

to become more conservative as you approach your retirement date. They may be useful for investors who really don't want to manage their investments, but many are quite expensive in terms of fees. They are also *too* cautious for you if you're already retired, as they won't produce a good income or keep your assets growing. So if you can find low-cost target date funds, trust your entire portfolio to them if you really don't want anything to do with money management; otherwise, you'd be better off with a 60:40 portfolio (60% equity, 40% bonds) using ETFs.

Annuities

An annuity is a contract between you and an insurance company. In return for your payment, the insurance company will pay out a regular income over your lifetime, or over a specific period. The insurer will assess your health, average mortality rates, and your life expectancy, and will price the annuity accordingly.

Annuities can be:

- **Fixed** – a given monthly or yearly payout.
- **Indexed** – a payout that is based on an index such as the S&P 500.
- **Variable** – basically a type of savings scheme in which you put money in over a period.

Buying an annuity can make good sense in creating a stable and reliable stream of income. Obviously, you want to check the financial health of the insurer, and it can be a good idea to have two or three different contracts. However, these are complex products. In the UK, most defined contribution pension funds are used to buy an annuity. Often, the plan provider will offer its own annuity, but you have the right to shop around, since rates can vary widely.

Annuities are used in the US as savings schemes. During the accumulation phase, you invest, and during the payout phase, you receive an income based on your investment gains as well as your contributions. They are not suitable for short-term savings, as the costs are often high and there are substantial penalties for early withdrawal.

Inheritance

If you are lucky, you may inherit funds. In the US, inherited funds are not federally taxed, though there is an estate tax on funds over $12.92m. In the UK, inheritance tax is payable on estates over £325,000 (or £500,000 when a house is left to children or grandchildren), except for money left to a surviving spouse or civil partner.

However, once you have inherited funds, you will pay tax on any future income or capital gains, unless you invest the funds in a tax-deferred or tax-exempt vehicle.

Home equity

Home equity can be a way to free up funds for retirement. In France, there's a specific way to do this called a *viager* – the owner sells their house for a 'bouquet' (down-payment) which is way below the market price, plus regular cash installments for the rest of their life. They continue to live in the house. The purchaser is making something of a gamble: if the owner lives to the ripe old age of 122 (as one Frenchwoman, Jeanne Calment, did!), they may lose money.

In the US, freeing up home equity can be done in various ways. A home equity loan gives you a lump sum of cash, but you must start to repay the loan (and pay interest) immediately. A home equity line of credit (HELOC), on the other hand, allows you to take funds during the draw period; no interest is charged till you make use of the facility. Unlike a home equity loan, which is fixed-rate, a HELOC is a variable-rate loan, which exposes you to potential increases in interest rates. You can get these in both the UK and the US.

UK lenders offer a lifetime mortgage. This works in a similar way to the *viager*, but is offered by a finance company, not an individual. You'll need to take specialized financial advice before you get a lifetime mortgage. A big downside is that your ability to move home in future (e.g. to a retirement complex) could be limited and you can end up owing the bank the full value of your house on your death. The lenders will have a minimum age after which you can take out a lifetime mortgage – generally over fifty-five.

A simpler way of freeing up home equity is to downsize or relocate to a cheaper area. This has the big advantage that selling your home is tax-efficient, with no capital gains tax charged in the UK where it has been your home throughout ownership and no tax for the first $250,000 of profit ($500,000 for a married couple) in the US. You'll need to consider this decision carefully. Can you find a smaller property in the same area, for instance? Do you feel open to making new friends and contacts in a different area when you retire? And if you're moving abroad, think carefully about whether you might want to return and what impact that would have on your life, and particularly on your tax affairs.

How volatile are these investments?

You'll need to think about how volatile your various investments are; that is, how much the price of the investment can vary over the short term. For instance, individual stocks can gain or lose 10% in a single day. The market as a whole is less volatile; if you bought ETFs rather than trying to pick individual stocks, you would generally see less extreme price movements.

But even so, when you consider that the Nasdaq 100 fell 20% in 2022, you can see that stocks are volatile. In the medium or longer term, stocks show the best returns, but to get those returns, you need to be able to take a certain amount of risk. While you could easily commit 100% of your funds to equities in your twenties and thirties, later in life you may want to think about expanding your real estate and bond holdings.

Real estate tends to be less volatile than equity. However, that depends on the type of real estate – residential or commercial – and on development/ new-build trends. Too much development together with a weakened economy can cause prices to fall. However, in most cases, holders of investment real estate will continue to see a stream of rental income and prices generally bounce back.

Bonds are generally considered less volatile than equity. As with real estate, you need to be careful to specify what type of bond you're buying. Low-credit-rating corporate bonds ('junk bonds') are likely to behave more like equity, while US government bonds are considerably less volatile. Longer-duration bonds (e.g., twenty-year treasuries) will be more volatile than shorter duration bonds. Bonds with less than a year to maturity (repayment) are unlikely to see much price movement at all.

Bonds are not 100% 'safe' though. Their prices vary inversely with interest rates. In plain language, when interest rates fall, bond prices go up, and when interest rates go up, bond prices fall. A good example of the latter was what happened to bonds in 2022 as the Fed hiked rates to stem inflation – US Treasury prices fell 12%. However, that was truly exceptional; the worst two years for bonds, apart from 2022, have seen price declines of only 2%.

As well as thinking about volatility, you'll also need to think about liquidity – that is, how easy it is to exit an investment. For instance, residential real estate is less volatile than stocks, but it is significantly less liquid. You may not be able to sell when you want to and the process takes significantly more time than clicking 'sell' on your broker's website. Thinking about liquidity also applies to the way you hold your investments. Are you able to transfer them easily between providers, for instance?

Try to keep your emotions at bay when you're assessing volatility. 'Risk' can be a very triggering word, particularly when you see a warning that "You could lose all your capital." If you have diversified your investments, for instance by buying funds rather than stocks, it is extremely unlikely that you will lose everything. However, you do need to assess rationally what amount of capital loss would severely impact your retirement. If you are in your twenties, even if the stock market fell 30%, you have forty years to get your money back. If you are sixty-four and wanted to retire next year, the same fall in the market could mean you'll have to dial back your lifestyle aspirations or keep working for a couple of years.

How much will you need?

Remember that retirement income refers to all the income you receive, not just a pension. It will include any government pension to which you're entitled, any workplace pension, and any retirement plan you have subscribed to. It will also include any investment income, for instance from a brokerage account or rental property, and any income from continued employment. If you have passive income such as royalties, that should be included too.

Add that all up. Do you have enough? That's a bit of a "how long is a piece of string" question, so let's unpick it.

- Have you paid off your home loan? Do you have any other debts that need to be repaid?
- What are your lifestyle aspirations? What will you want to spend money on – travel, entertainment, a boat, a sport? Or do you just want to live quietly in your old home?

You'll want your income (after tax) to last a good few decades, so think hard before taking capital out of your plan. Can you live just on the investment income? It may well be that your 401k and social security entitlements will give you enough to live on. If not, you need to save more, or identify another type of income (such as taking home equity).

Chapter Five

DEBT, TAXES, AND THE LEGAL STUFF

There is a lot of debt around. More than sixty-four million Americans carry credit card debt (some at worrying levels), according to the Urban Institute. Many more than that hold home or car loans, business or personal loans, or other forms of debt. In spring 2021, the Federal Reserve said American household debt had hit a record $14.6 trillion; a CNBC report showed that the *average* American had $90,460 in debt.

Most worrying for your retirement prospects is that, according to the Fed, many more seniors now have a home loan than did thirty years ago. Over a third of those between sixty-five and seventy-four still have a mortgage, against just over 20% three decades ago, and 20% of over-seventy-fives still have an outstanding home loan, against less than 10% in 1989. The average amount outstanding has increased, too, from about $20,000 to just below $100,000 (and that is much more than the adjusted inflation amount – $20,000 in 1989 is worth around $48,253 in 2023)

Common forms of debt

Let's take a look at some of the more common forms of debt.

Credit cards

Credit cards are the most common form of debt for seniors. A credit card can be a very helpful means of payment and offers significant protection against fraud. It's also easier to dispute unauthorized purchases or purchases of goods lost or damaged in shipping than with a debit card.

However, credit cards make it very easy to spend money you don't have. They account for 55% of all US debt, and according to a survey by Clever, 67% of retirees have a balance on credit cards that they haven't managed to pay off. If you have a bad record of falling into temptation, then you need to think about reducing your reliance on credit cards before you retire. On the other hand, if you have always been able to pay off your full balance, month by month, you're probably not going to have an issue (though remember that you'll probably need to cope with doing so on a reduced income).

Credit cards are one of the most expensive forms of debt, so it may be worth consolidating your debt before retirement. Move your balance to a 0% credit card or take out a personal loan. This will reduce your interest rate and make it easier to pay off the balance.

Mortgage

We often think of mortgages as being something that you'll pay off before retirement, but for a third of pensioners, this is no longer the case. Make it a priority to clear your debt before you retire if you can. It's not always possible; if you lose your job in your late fifties, and end up taking a less well remunerated position, you might not be able to. But it's clearly easier to adjust to a lower income, and potentially higher medical bills, if you don't have a loan to pay off.

Home loans generally have a low rate of interest, so if you have credit card bills, pay those off first. However, the risk of having a home loan is that if you're unable to pay, you could lose your home. Apart from avoiding financial stress, such as not being able to pay bills, paying off your mortgage before retirement removes a major source of emotional worry.

Good debt

Is debt always 'bad'? It's worth pointing out that debt has several advantages. For instance, by taking out a home loan, you are able to invest in your own home and that should produce an equity return as real estate prices increase. Debt taken out to grow a business can also produce positive returns.

Some investors use debt to create leverage that can improve their returns. For instance, they buy stocks 'on margin,' putting down only half the price in cash. As long as markets go up, this can vastly improve returns. However, if the stock price falls, the remaining 50% has to be paid, and if you can't pay up, the broker can sell the stock, crystallizing a loss. Leveraged ETFs offer to pay double or triple what the S&P 500 makes in gains. Again, the downside is that if the market falls, you'll see the ETF shrink by two or three times the market. While such techniques may work for experienced professional investors, the risk profile is uncomfortably high for most, and basic math suggests that over the long term, leveraged ETFs will underperform the market (a doubled loss requires more than double the return to make good).

Other liabilities

Other forms of debt may include all your various bills and other commitments, such as subscriptions, corporate loans, and charitable giving. It can be hard to reduce these commitments, particularly if you feel you are letting people down, for instance if you have to cut your contributions to a local charity or sports club. However, you may need to look at the total regular payments you make and see if they can be cut. Assess the value you get out of a gym membership, for instance, and look at alternative packages. Once you no longer have to go to work, you can go to the gym in off-peak hours and get a senior discount, for instance.

You may have a number of subscriptions that you don't use much. For instance, a friend had been paying to be a member of the National Trust for years. When she retired, she decided she would either use her free access to UK National Trust historic properties or give up the membership. She is now on her 102nd property and has, over the last couple of years, seen medieval castles, Bridgerton-style stately homes, and John Lennon's childhood home.

Medical bills

These are something you'll need to take into account. Eighty percent of seniors have one or more long-term conditions that need treatment. You'll also likely need more regular check-ups as you get older. If your medical plans don't cover these treatments and check-ups, your retirement fund will have to finance them.

In the UK, most medical care is free, though having medical insurance can help bypass long queues for surgery such as hip replacements, and some kinds of treatment, such as chiropody, are not included. However, in the US, Medicare only covers a certain amount of your bills, so you'll need another insurance policy to pay the excess.

RBC Wealth Management estimates a *healthy* sixty-five-year-old in the US is likely to need $404,253 over the rest of their lifetime to cover medical bills. That excludes long-term care costs, which run up to $100,000 a year. By age seventy-five, 15% of your income may be spent on medical costs. You need to factor that into your planning. You'll also want to factor in the fact that medical costs are growing at about 5% a year, as new technology and increased patient expectations drive costs higher.

Retirement taxes

Taxes in retirement are easy to forget – until you need to pay them! While a Roth 401k or Roth IRA will give you tax-free income, regular 401ks (and in the UK, SIPPs and other pensions) will be taxable. You do have a little leeway, as taxes are only payable in the tax year that you take income. So, if you are in control of how much you take (e.g., with income drawdown in the UK), and when, you can decide to stay within a given tax bracket for the year once you've allowed for any other income.

If you're in the US, remember that while federal income tax is standard, state taxes on retirement income vary by state. You pay tax to the state where you are living in retirement, even if you earned the money elsewhere. For federal taxes, the IRS provides a useful guide to retirement benefits (Publication 915), and the Tax Guide for Seniors (Publication 554) – both are available on the IRS website.

Many older Americans are surprised to learn they might have to pay tax on part of the social security income they receive, if their *overall* income exceeds a certain amount. Whether you have to pay such taxes will depend on how much overall retirement income you and your spouse receive, and whether you file joint or separate tax returns. Publication 915 will give you the base income amounts – the higher that total, the greater part of your benefits will be taxable. It can range from 50 to 85% depending on your income, and you won't get any tax breaks if you're married and file separate returns.

Note that to get tax-free income from your Roth IRA, you must have had the account for five years or more. So if you have investments in stocks, it might well be worth swapping them into your Roth IRA in the years coming up to your expected retirement date – over a decade, you'd be able to shelter a total of $75,000. A Roth 401k started at fifty can accept $27,000 a year, so that's over a quarter of a million dollars of investment sheltered by the time you're sixty, providing tax-free income in your retirement.

In the UK, ISAs are tax-exempt. But investment income that comes from non-ISA accounts is taxable, including both capital gains and dividends or interest. However, you should be able to utilize the current tax-free amounts of £12,570 (for income tax) and £6,000 (for capital gains – this will reduce to £3,000 from 6 April 2024).

You can also reduce your rate of tax by using investments which have tax breaks attached. In the UK, investing in Venture Capital Trusts has an up-front tax break for new subscriptions and it's also worth noting that VCTs bought on the stock market have capital gains and income tax exemptions, and some have quite high yields. However, these are relatively high-risk investments and only for the wealthier and more street-wise investor. In the US, municipal bonds are also exempt from federal tax, and if you buy munis (municipal bonds) from your own state, those will be exempt from state taxes, too.

If you are saving in taxable accounts, and are in the US, there are a few ways to economize on taxes. For instance, if you hold a stock more than sixty-one days before it pays a dividend, 'qualified' dividends are taxed at the long-term capital gains rate, which is lower than the income tax rates. If you keep a stock more than a year, you'll pay the long-term capital gains rate (0 or 20% depending on your other income) when you sell. And you can, of course, crystallize losses on your poorly performing stocks to set against your capital gains.

Legal considerations

Power of Attorney

Legal considerations are something you'll want to think about. We all think "I'm not going any time soon," but as you approach retirement age, you'll want to think about making a power of attorney (POA) in case you lose your ability to manage your financial affairs for whatever reason. If your home and brokerage account are only in your name, your spouse would need a POA to take any actions relating to them, like selling them, if you weren't able to make your own decisions (e.g., through dementia or hospitalization).

It's important you get this done ahead of time, because a POA can't be set up if the principal no longer has sufficient mental capacity - and it is the principal who needs to set up the POA. Your family can't do it for you. If you are incapacitated without a POA, a court has to appoint a guardian or conservator; you won't have any choice over who is appointed, and costs are likely to be high.

Inheritance

You'll also want to think about what inheritance you are leaving to children, grandchildren, maybe your university or an arts venue or a charitable foundation. Looking after family and good friends is usually the most important thing on people's minds, and there are various things you can do to make things easier.

It can often be a good idea to make substantial gifts while you are still here to do it. Every year, you can give $17,000 tax free (each) to any number of donees if you're in the US. If you are married, you each have that $17,000 allowance, so between the two of you, you could give your children $34,000 each. These gifts will reduce the amount of taxable estate that you leave when you die. On the other hand, if you need money later in retirement, you may have to borrow it from your children.

Transferring assets to your children before you die can make very good sense. Emotionally, it lets you see how they are using your gifts. For instance, if you have a child or grandchild who wants to build their own house or needs to spend money on a professional-level musical instrument to go to the Juillard conservatoire, you'll get so much fun out of seeing the difference that your gift has made. It may also be useful in assessing whether your children or grandchildren can manage their money properly. But it can also make good sense financially. For instance, if you transfer a holiday home, you no longer have to pay property taxes on it. And if you transfer an apartment, say, for your youngest to live in, there will be no capital gains tax for you to pay if its value increases once you've handed it over.

There are other rules for larger gifts over your lifetime; IRS Form 709 has notes which explain these. The rules are quite strict and it's important to comply.

The UK is much less generous: you can only give £3,000 a year, though you can roll this over for a year (i.e., the year two allowance would be £6,000), but you can only do so once. You can give gifts above this amount in what's called a Potentially Exempt Transfer (PET), but if you die within seven years, it will be added to your estate and the recipients will have to pay inheritance tax on it if your estate is above the threshold for tax.

Trusts

Trusts are another way of passing on your wealth. They can make sense if you have a child who has an addiction, debts, or other issues, since the trust retains the assets and pays the individual an income, managing the assets on their behalf. An irrevocable trust can also take your assets out of your ownership, so they can no longer be claimed by creditors or by Medicaid. A blind trust can be established for children or grandchildren that will mature once they reach twenty-one or graduate from college.

Another type of trust that some US families choose is a Generation-Skipping Trust, which passes assets directly to grandchildren, thus avoiding estate taxes that the children would otherwise need to pay. A Qualified Personal Residence Trust allows you to gift the ownership of your home, while retaining the right to live in it. Just about the only thing you can't put in a trust is an IRA.

Trusts work similarly in the UK, though the details are different. To establish one, you'll need expert legal help, and they are generally only worth considering for wealthier families, or in the case of disabled children who need the money to be managed for them. There is a fairly high cost to setting up trusts, so make sure they are worth it before you start.

Types of trust in the US	
Qualified Personal Residence Trust	Removes your principal residence from the value of your estate, while allowing you to live in it for a period
Charitable Lead Trust	An irrevocable trust set up in favor of a charity, giving the donor access to various tax breaks and reducing the amount of the estate

Types of trust in the US	
Insurance Trust	An irrevocable trust set up to hold a life insurance policy, keeping the proceeds of the policy out of your estate
Generation-Skipping Trust	A trust which passes down assets to grandchildren, 'skipping' a generation and avoiding the payment of two sets of estate taxes
Special Needs Trust	A trust that is set up to help supplement a disabled or chronically ill person's income, without their losing eligibility for public assistance programs
Credit Shelter Trust	A trust that can help affluent couples minimize estate tax; each spouse creates a trust in which their assets are held, allowing the other spouse to access the assets held in trust, without taking ownership and thus without increasing the amount of that spouse's estate
Blind Trust	A trust established giving another party control of assets. Often used when an individual wants to avoid conflicts of interest; the beneficiaries and trustor don't know what assets are in the trust
Qualified Terminable Property Interest Trust	Allows assets to be held in trust for a surviving spouse; determines what will happen to the assets on that spouse's death. Helpful in dealing with families where there are children from previous marriages
Separate Share Trust	Can be used to ensure that a child or grandchild with problems such as addiction, debts, or in the middle of a divorce, does not lose the assets, and that the assets are administered for their benefit

Chapter Six

WHY YOU MUST GET AHEAD IN SAVING FOR RETIREMENT

Maybe you've read this far and you're still not convinced that you really need to prioritize retirement saving *right now*. You have other things you want to do. You have young kids and you want to give them the best opportunities in childhood – perhaps opportunities that you yourself didn't have. Or you want to travel the world before you're stuck in a career with a home loan to pay off. Or you looked at a retirement scheme, but it would mean locking your money up for too long, and you want to start your own business in ten years or so. Or you started your own business, and it's a struggle, and you don't have enough time to worry about investing...

There are always plenty of reasons to procrastinate when it comes to retirement saving. So this chapter is about the reasons you really must not put it off. If you like, this chapter is about giving you the right motivation to save.

Reasons to start now

You will still have bills to pay but you have dreams, too

You want to do things when you're retired that you didn't have the chance to do when you were working. You may want to travel, build a new house, or play in a rock band.

If you retire with just social security, you may never achieve your dreams. If your 401k is underfunded, you may end up worrying about money instead of enjoying your new life. Don't give up on your dreams – fund your 401k instead.

You need money to fund liabilities

If the carrot of living your dreams didn't work, try the stick of "I still have to pay maintenance to my ex-wife." Or you'll still be paying off your home loan when you retire. Or you need to fund your own medical insurance. None of this is going to be easy unless you have a retirement income that covers it.

You want freedom

You may have spent years at someone else's beck and call. You may not have enjoyed it. Your career may have ended up boring you or didn't turn out the way you'd thought it would. If you've saved up enough, you can buy your freedom. Even if it is your employer who puts money in your pension pot, it's now *your* money, and you decide what to do with it.

You can choose how to invest that money. And to quite a large extent, you can choose how you take that money – as a lump sum, as a regular annuity pension, or just dipping into the 'pot' from time to time.

You can retire early

Okay, maybe it helps if you are Michael Jordan or Justin Bieber. But it's not a daydream, even if you're not a basketball player or a rockstar. I know someone who retired before he was forty. He worked very hard in his early twenties and put all the money he could into buying a portfolio of rented properties. Those properties now supply his retirement income.

The earlier you start saving and investing, the more likely it is that you'll be able to retire early. Your money will have been invested for longer if you retire at sixty or sixty-five, and you'll enjoy the positive impact of compounding, your wealth increasing in size like a snowball.

You'll get a clear sense of direction

As you watch your investments grow, you can see how they are headed somewhere. Of course, unless you are a finance whiz or a professional, you'll probably want to get some help with your asset allocation and investment management, for instance using a robo-advisor, rather than picking stocks based on what you see on TV.

In fact, if you're investing in stocks, you're helping the economy by putting your money to work. Without the stock market, companies would lose access to one of the main ways they can raise finance. Yes, they'd still be able to secure loans and private companies can issue shares, but they wouldn't get the same reach as they do with a public stock market, which much of the world has easy access to. If you're investing in real estate, particularly if you're involved in refurbishment, you're helping people find a home to live in or a space to carry out their business activities.

You'll have less to argue with your partner about

Money is a big reason for marriage and relationship breakdowns; it's cited in about 40% of all divorces in the US. Sometimes, a couple agree that they need to save for retirement, but one of them doesn't play ball – taking money out of savings, spending too much, or refusing to set specific goals. That's particularly bad news when there's not quite enough income to go around – which will be the case in retirement, unless you do something about it now! Knowing your retirement is well covered will also reduce stress levels, as you have much less need to worry about the future.

You'll have a retirement that actually feels like retirement

No one can threaten to cut your pay or fire you; your retirement income is secure. You'll have enough money *and* enough time to do what you want to do. You can live your best life, or maybe fulfill a childhood dream.

When you put money into your retirement funds, you're doing your future-self a big favor. It might be difficult to imagine yourself at sixty. The odds are you'll have had a lot of experiences that have changed you, but deep down you'll still be driven by the same interests and desires you have now. So shake hands with your future-self and make sure that person has everything they need to make their retirement a success!

You'll be able to leave a legacy

Whether you want to leave a legacy to children and grandchildren, fund a charitable foundation, put up a commemorative bench at a local beauty spot, or leave your lovingly restored historic house to a local conservation group, if your retirement income is sorted, you'll be able to do it. If you've been dipping into your savings to help pay the bills because your social security doesn't go far enough, forget it.

It may be easier than you think to save

Don't get scared off because you don't understand stocks and shares, day-trading or advanced options theory. You don't need to. Use a robo-advisor, use a financial advisor, just buy ETFs in a brokerage account – there are loads of low-maintenance ways of investing. Or you could invest in real estate if that's something you know more about.

If you're a woman, you need to look after yourself

In the old days – grandma's days, or even great-grandma's – women didn't need pensions, as their husband's pension would cover them for life. Things have changed, but they haven't changed enough. A lot of women end up in pension poverty because of years spent looking after children or working part time, making no or low pension contributions.

So it's even more important to get started early if you're female. If you're coming up to retirement age and you've missed contributions for some years, it's worth assessing what you can do now. Use the catch-up IRA and 401k contribution levels if you can and see if you can 'purchase' extra years' contributions for an employer's or state pension. In the UK, if you don't think you will have contributed National Insurance for enough qualifying years (you currently need thirty-five full years to get the full state pension), because you have had time off to raise a family or have lived outside of the UK, you can make top-up voluntary contributions for those years.

Chapter Seven

SAVING THE OLD WAY AND HOW TO START MAKING YOUR MONEY WORK FOR YOU

Before money, people bartered. Some people held wealth in the form of cattle herds, others in the form of precious or semi-precious stones or precious metals. For instance, Bedouin women's jewelry wasn't just an adornment but a way to store wealth safely in a nomadic culture.

Once money was invented, things changed (though Bedouin women stuck to tradition, drilled holes through silver coins and hung them on their necklaces). But keeping money safe was hard. Some people dug holes in the ground and put their money there, others constructed huge wooden and iron chests with multiple locks. My grandma kept money under the mattress; she didn't trust banks.

Children even today have piggy banks. Although they're mostly in the shape of a pig, the phrase 'piggy bank' actually derives from the medieval *pygg*, which is the kind of clay that money-holding pots were made of.

While banks existed before the 19th century, they were only for wealthy people; most working people got paid (and saved) in cash. The first chartered bank in the USA was incorporated in 1816 as the Provident Institution for Savings, headquartered in Boston, MA. Since then, banks have become where we store our money – in cash or, increasingly, in dematerialized form.

You may think that 'putting money in the bank' is a good thing. Society values 'saving' and our parents tell us to save, and we grow up thinking that putting money into a bank account is the same thing as putting money in a piggy bank.

In fact, this is one of the biggest confidence tricks that's ever been played. When you put money in the bank, even if it's earning a small rate of interest, your money is probably losing its purchasing power through inflation. You're not getting a real return (that is, a return above inflation). In fact, you may even be paying your bank for the privilege.

Your money ought to be working for *you* and the only way to make it do this is to buy value-creating assets, whether those are stocks, bonds, or properties. The only money you need to put in the bank is the money you need immediate access to for daily spending and perhaps a rainy-day fund to cover unexpected expenses.

In fact, if you invest enough, and wisely, you could become financially independent. Oddly enough, that's something that society often doesn't seem to value. You keep hearing that you ought to get a 'good job,' you ought to work for someone else, you ought to have a 'steady salary.' It's sometimes difficult being an entrepreneur when your mother still wishes you had become a doctor or a lawyer!

So let's take the first steps to making your money work for you, instead of you working for your money.

Make your money work for you

First steps

While the bank is a good first home for your 'spare' money and savings, make sure that your money doesn't stay there too long. Find a way to invest it so that you can grow your savings in real terms. You will need to take a longer-term approach to investment than you can with savings, but even if you're saving up for buying your own home in a few years' time, it's worth putting some of your money to work, or you might never get there.

Your first step should be to find a way of investing automatically. For instance, if you decide you want to use a robo-advisor, set up an automated payment the day after you get your salary in your bank account. You can do the same for most investments, though if you use a broker, you'll need to log on once the money's there in order to invest it.

You may not be aware of all the different options that you have for investing, so here are some ideas.

Social investing

This can be a way of putting your social conscience to work, together with your funds. You might, for instance, invest through crowdfunding in small, women-owned businesses. You might choose 'impact investing,' a form of investing that concentrates on making a social or environmental impact as well as a financial return; sustainable agriculture, renewable energy, and microfinance are all areas you might look at. You might look at CNote, which is focused on community investing.

Remember, though, that you may need to keep money in these investments for a given period before you can sell. For instance, CNote offers thirty-month and sixty-month investments, the Flagship Fund and the Wisdom Fund. These offer 3% a year interest and 1% a year respectively, so they are not hugely profitable investments, but you will get some return on your funds.

You might also put some or all of your funds into environmental, social and governance (ESG) funds, or decide to invest in companies which have values or create products or provide services you support, such as offering financial services to African-American communities, actively supporting women in management, or developing renewable energies.

An easy way to invest in ESG companies without having to do a load of research is to buy an ETF like Vanguard's ESG US Stock ETF (ESGV) or its international sibling VSGX, or the iShares Global Clean Energy ETF (ICLN). These vet companies according to a scoring system, so they won't invest in companies that are unethical or that are big polluters.

Virtual banking

Virtual banking will usually deliver you higher interest rates on your cash than a traditional branch bank. Monzo or Starling Bank in the UK, and Bread Financial or Synchrony in the US, offer better rates on savings than most of the big banks. Move your savings into one of these banks and you're adding a little extra return, though you will still need other investments.

Tangible assets

Purchase tangible assets that generate cash flow. The obvious example of this is rental apartments or single-family homes, which offer a higher yield than savings (if they don't in your particular area, house prices are too high). But you could also buy other assets such as garages, vending machines, or self-storage sites; farmland and forest can also be good investments if you are wealthy (or through a collective investment fund). However, you'll need to do some work, particularly ensuring that you research the opportunity properly and know exactly what you are doing.

Foreign currency

This can be a focus for investment. However, currencies are extremely volatile and you really need to understand the risk profile. Generally, most people involved in currency are traders, not investors. Take expert advice before you get involved.

Remember that foreign currencies don't pay dividends and can be very volatile. Typically, they may move very fast over a period as short as a couple of minutes. This isn't the kind of long-term investment you want for a retirement fund.

It is more important to understand that if you are investing in foreign stocks, you will be incurring some currency risk. That's particularly the case with emerging markets but can apply to highly developed markets too. For instance, if you'd invested $1,000 in euros in 2014, you'd have got €1,190 for it, while $1,000 invested today would get just €1000 (in early 2023). In other words, your investments would be working against a significant currency headwind. Some funds will attempt to hedge the currency exposure, so that you get the returns while minimizing the headwind; make sure you know whether any fund you buy is hedged or unhedged. A hedged fund will minimize short-term ups and downs.

One time it really pays to think about currency is if you know you will be retiring to another country. Cuenca, Ecuador, is quite a popular retirement destination. If you're an American retiring there, you don't need to worry, as the official currency there is the US dollar. But if you were going to retire in Europe and you don't want dollar-euro volatility to affect your monthly income, you might want to think about having more euro assets in the portfolio.

Crowdfunding

Crowdfunding can be an interesting way to put small amounts of money to work. It's a way of using technology to connect individual lenders with borrowers, so the 'crowd,' not a bank, decides whether to fund a loan. Most crowdfunding is lending based, offering loans to small businesses or to property developments which pay a higher rate of interest than you would get from bank savings. Some real estate crowdfunding pays 8 to 9% a year, while being secured on a first lien (a legal right or claim against a property – like a mortgage), giving it relatively robust security. Other crowdfunding platforms allow you to invest equity seed capital in small businesses; you'll get paid a percentage of the profits – if there are any.

There are four main types of platform:

- **Crowdlending/peer-to-peer lending**.
- **Donation based** – this is not popular, but sites like Kiva (charitable micro-loans) enable you to do a lot of good by lending on a non-interest paying basis, while GoFundMe lets you fund charitable causes.
- **Equity based** – taking a stake in real estate or a company. If things go wrong, you'll be paid last, but this has potential for high rewards.
- **Reward based** – you get no shares in the business, but you are entitled to certain benefits (e.g., on Kickstarter).

While you can use these platforms to raise money (e.g., if you're a house flipper or have your own business), we're looking here at how you can use them to invest.

Crowdfunding is good for fundraisers, since banks may not be interested in lending to them. That could be because they have a bad business model and their business plan looks poor, but it might simply be because their project is too small for banks to be interested or doesn't fit commercial banks' norms (for instance, house flipping is not something most banks will consider). This gives you as an investor access to areas of the economy you might not otherwise be able to invest in, such as small, high-growth businesses or office real estate.

Pure peer-to-peer lending allows individuals lend to other individuals, but this is no longer where most investors go. Instead, crowdfunding platforms feature corporate loans in which individuals can invest. The platform will usually look at borrowers' creditworthiness, sometimes attributing it a rating so you can see the degree of risk involved, and then open the loan to individual investors.

But you'll need to do some due diligence, because some of these projects are not great. Ensure the management team has a track record of success, and make sure the project is legitimate (check out the area on Google maps if you're crowdfunding a house flip, for instance).

You'll also need to ensure you get a return that's better than the return on alternative investments. Broadly, you're looking at 9% upwards; some say 11-15%. And even if you have a good appetite for risk, don't put more than 10% of your total funds in crowdfunding.

Real estate crowdfunding can be a good way to invest. A crowdfunding platform pools investors' money to buy a property or to fund a development or renovation. Typically, the owners of the project will contribute some funds ('skin in the game'), a large percentage will come from traditional commercial banking, and the crowdfunding will account for a slice of perhaps 5% or 10%. This gives individuals access to big-ticket deals they couldn't otherwise afford; New York office buildings, for instance, sell for millions, but you can get involved via a crowdfund.

Returns are then shared between the investors. For an equity crowdfund, you'll be getting a share of rental income, while a loan investment will give you interest, generally at a relatively high rate. You may get paid monthly, quarterly, or simply through a 'balloon payment' at the end of the loan term.

The keys to success are choosing a good and reputable platform and working out your criteria for investment. For instance, in my own portfolio, I will only make loans to developments that are 45% or more pre-sold, and where my investment is protected by a warranty or a first lien. I have no loans in default, and only two that are paying interest while delaying repayment by a few months – not bad considering they couldn't work on site during Covid lockdowns. You'll also want to ensure you build a diverse set of projects rather than putting all your money into one. If you find one developer has consistently delivered for you, it's worth making a note and backing their future projects.

Crowdfunding sites where you could start might include Crowd Street, Equity Multiple, FundRise, and PeerStreet; in France, Anaxago and Koregraf in the US; and Property Partner, CrowdProperty, CapitalRise and LendInvest in the UK.

Diversifying

Remember to diversify. You can take more risk in your twenties and thirties, but if you're picking higher-risk investments, you should manage your risk by diversifying. So, for instance, you might split investments between crowdfunded real estate, US small caps, and emerging markets. These are all relatively higher-risk investments, but it's unlikely that all three will underperform at the same time.

Many brokers will suggest particular portfolios for given investor styles or requirements. A good example of how these might add up is shown in the table below.

Aggressive/dynamic	Moderate / balanced	Conservative
30% international equity	40% bonds	60% long-term bonds
45% domestic large caps	35% domestic large cap	20% short-term bonds
15% domestic small and mid-cap	15% international	20% domestic large cap equity
10% emerging markets	10% domestic small and mid-cap	

Of course, this only shows the allocation for equity and bond holdings. If you also owned a rental apartment and had some crowdfunding loans running, you'd be even better diversified.

Chapter Eight

SET YOUR RETIREMENT ON FIRE

FIRE has become a widespread acronym in financial circles (and we've already mentioned it in an earlier chapter; you can't write about retirement these days without mentioning it). The initials stand for Financial Independence / Retire Early, and while some of its adherents have adopted rather extreme measures to retire in their 30s (why eat sandwiches from trash cans when you're earning $95,000 a year?), it's not just a lunatic fringe idea. There's a lot more to it than that.

Let's ignore the 'retire early' part; FIRE is all about financial independence. For instance, you might want to have enough money that you can walk out of a job you find uninspiring or take a year or two to travel the world (that might well go with becoming a digital nomad rather than just giving up paid work). Or you can carry on working but know you're doing so because you want to, not just to pay the bills. Having what's sometimes called 'F.U. Money' means no more worries about what happens if your firm has to make layoffs or you get a new boss you can't stand and want to leave.

Or you could decide to give up a highly-paid job when burnout looms, and do something less remunerative but about which you're passionate, like woodworking, running a craft brewery, or working in a charity. In short, FIRE is all about freedom.

For most FIRE practitioners, freedom is defined as twenty-five times your annual salary or annual expenses. If you take out 4% of your capital a year, you should be able to keep living off your capital indefinitely, as the rest of the portfolio will generate income and growth to replace that sum. This basic math underpins FIRE, and it's a lot easier to understand than a full discounted cash flow financial model, which is one reason it's become popular.

Back in 1992, Vicki Robin and Joe Dominguez wrote the book Your Money or Your Life. It took a while for the concept to catch FIRE (pun intended); blogs such as Mr Money Mustache and JL Collins, as well as Reddit forums, popularized the idea and by 2018, it had become mainstream.

The nitty-gritty of FIRE

FIRE is about achieving financial independence by living below your means (spending less than what you earn) and having a high level of savings. FIRE savers set aside as much as 70% of their monthly income for investment, usually investing in tracker funds and stocks. They avoid debt; usually, this includes housing loans unless they can pay them off within a few years.

FIRE can be summed up in a series of steps:

1. Save money.
2. Invest that money for higher returns.
3. Earn more money to invest.
4. Spend wisely (this may mean very frugally or ruthlessly prioritizing what you spend money on).

Save money

Saving money can involve living with extreme frugality. Some FIRE practitioners take this to extremes. They cut coupons, shop at thrift stores, go dumpster diving, and never eat out or take a vacation. They believe it's worth it if they get to trek around South America when they're in their thirties.

Don't forget other ways of reducing spending, such as using Black Friday and other sales when you need to make a big-ticket purchase, using coupons, using bulk buys to cut the cost of groceries, and even having 'no-spend' weeks. Having an automatic 'sweep' of your bank account to ensure money over a certain amount goes into interest-bearing accounts or your brokerage account is also a smart move; if money isn't there, you won't spend it.

Aggressive saving is certainly something that everyone can learn from the FIRE movement. Though it is not for everyone; if you're having difficulty paying basic expenses right now (and there are many people in that situation), then FIRE is not for you. Not now. Not yet.

Invest your money

Now let's talk about investment. Here again, FIRE overturns many conventional expectations, such as the 60/40 portfolio and 'putting money in the bank.' If you're pursuing FIRE, you must make higher-risk investment choices. For instance, you must put at least 70% of your portfolio into equity. You'll also need to invest in areas such as emerging markets, international equity, and value stocks to get higher returns than a DJIA or S&P500 portfolio would give you.

Where FIRE is a bit different from many financial outlooks is that many FIRE advocates don't consider owning their home an asset. If you have significant debt secured on your home, it's a liability because you have to keep paying out on it. It requires maintenance, the payment of property taxes, and insurance, so it's a net cost unless it's cheaper than renting the equivalent.

FIRE proponents would never agree with an estate agent telling them to "Buy the biggest house you can afford." They'd rather buy an adequate house than invest the rest of the money in the stock market or even rent if rental properties were cheaply available. On the other hand, they will invest in rental real estate - real estate that pays them an income.

Earn more money

Some people get started on FIRE but blow it when they get a raise. Suddenly, there's a load of extra money in their account, and they get used to having a bit more to spend. This is 'cost creep,' and you need to avoid it. If you have more money coming in, act immediately to get more going out - not in costs, but straight into your investment accounts. The higher your earnings, the more you can save from each month's paycheck.

Aiming to increase your earnings is the third step in FIRE. That might just be through asking for a raise. It might be through aggressively pursuing promotion opportunities, even if that means moving across the country. It might be through training courses to improve your skills or paying for a qualification that will allow you to move into a better-paying job in your profession; for instance, one legal secretary successfully put herself through a legal qualification enabling her to move across to the professional side.

If you've already committed to FIRE, taking time off to retrain is much easier as you'll already have a financial cushion. If taking an MBA would make sense, and you're already on the FIRE track, you can afford to quit your job and study. Just ensure you have a realistic idea of what it will cost and how much it will likely improve your earnings afterward.

Some FIRE followers increase their earnings by building a small business or holding down a second job. Side hustles could include writing textbooks or a software app, creating an authoritative blog, a dog walking business, or an Amazon or Etsy retail business. Just make sure you're not competing with your primary employer.

Increasing passive income by owning income-producing assets can also be a good FIRE strategy. For instance, real estate is a great income producer, though the entry ticket is high.

And then, of course, there's increasing your income by doing plenty of overtime and extra shifts. For lower-paid workers, this is the best way to earn more in the short term, but watch out for burnout.

Spend wisely

Others cut the cost of living by taking a ruthless approach to their housing. They live in vans or 'tiny houses' or buy a duplex to rent out half of it ('house hacking') and pay off their home loans (if they have any) as soon as possible.

If you don't earn much, you might need that kind of frugality to save anything at all. But most people can take a more relaxed attitude to reduce their costs. For instance, do you really need a car if you live in a city or in a suburb with good public transportation links? Using a car hire company when you're taking a trip might be significantly cheaper than the cost of insurance, a parking place, and car finance. Or you might just decide that even though most of your peers are driving new cars, you can cope with driving an older car and being its second or third owner.

You could cut the cost of your housing by having a smaller city apartment than you can actually afford. Or you might, if you want more space, compromise on the neighborhood; if you can work remotely, you might move right out into a rural area. You might also consider buying a home that needs some renovation.

What FIRE really teaches is mindfulness in spending. It can be helpful to think about how many hours it took to earn your car, your grocery bill, a restaurant meal, and a cappuccino every morning this week. You don't have to be stingy. If you really love your morning coffee, you don't necessarily need to give it up. $5 a coffee is $25 a week, which is $1300 a year; it's probably not enough on its own to make a significant difference in your life. Add it together with economizing on eating out, and a more cost-conscious grocery shop, though, and the savings could be a lot more.

On the other hand, not having a car could save you over $2,000 a year in maintenance costs, as well as your being able to put the capital you'd otherwise have spent into your pension fund. That is a more acceptable cut if you don't need a car.

Some FIRE devotees never take a vacation. For some people, though, they're not prepared to compromise on travel. They need to get out into nature or visit different cultures; it's important to them (this is me!). So they'll economize on the other living costs and then buy an RV or a small camper van or stay in hostels to afford their travel habit.

Avoiding debt is another thing everyone can learn from FIRE. That doesn't mean not using credit cards, which have certain advantages - points, rewards, and insurance on goods bought with them. It simply means paying the balance off monthly to avoid debt.

Different flavors of FIRE

FIRE comes in several different flavors. Traditional FIRE is simply about building up a pot of investments which lets you withdraw passive income whenever you need. But there are also various sub-categories.

- **Fat FIRE** is about aiming to enjoy the good life with passive income of $100-200,000 per year, and that requires very high investment. Fat FIRE is for high earners only, and if your tastes are simple and your desires limited, it's not necessary for you.
- **Barista FIRE** is about saving a smaller 'pot' but complementing your early retirement by taking on a 'fun' job such as barista, diving instructor, or mountain guide.
- **Coast FIRE** is not about being a beach bum but about 'coasting' to retirement. With Coast FIRE, you aim to build your pot up to the point at which investment returns should enable you to reach your target without any fresh investment on your part. You then 'coast,' no longer needing to contribute but not withdrawing any income.
- **Lean FIRE** is the most aggressively frugal, minimalist path. It's about cutting your expenditure as far as you can. Some people hate it. Other people find it enhances the Zen in their lives.

So there's nothing to stop you from creating your own subcategory of FIRE. As long as you're achieving financial independence, it doesn't matter whether you've invented "Carry on working as a hot-shot lawyer FIRE" or

"Retire to my Side Hustle FIRE"...

What you need for FIRE

Let's say your plan is to use the FIRE program to retire at forty. It's possible, but it's not going to be easy. First of all, you'll need a reasonably paid job or one which offers you the chance of significant paid overtime working. Secondly, you'll need a lot of self-discipline.

And thirdly, you need to do the basic math I mentioned at the start of the chapter. If you want to retire on a $40,000/year income, multiply that by twenty-five to get the size of the investment pot you need. That means you'll need a $1m investment portfolio. Even living on a very frugal income in retirement, retiring early takes a significant investment.

That would probably require investing $32,000 a year and getting 7-8% investment returns. Obviously, that's really hard to do if you only earn $50,000, while earning $120,000, it's much easier!

What is great about FIRE is that the math is so easy. There's also a supportive community around the internet, so if you accept the challenge, you'll have many peers cheering you on.

The best investments for FIRE

One of the problems with early retirement is that the state will not make it easy for you. State schemes, and tax breaks, are organized so that you retire at the usual time like everyone else. So if you actually want to retire at forty, you'll need to invest in something other than a pension, as the earliest you can claim your pension is fifty-five in the US and the UK (and this will shortly rise to fifty-seven in the UK). In the US, it's not particularly tax-efficient to access a pension before the age of fifty-nine and a half, though it can be done.

The problem is that more flexible investments may not be as tax-efficient as pensions; they're also not as well ring-fenced in retirement. So it is probably best to use a mixture of pension and other investments.

In the UK, ISAs offer you a flexible way to save that's highly tax efficient. You can put £20,000 (at present) every tax year into ISAs, and there is no limit on the total amount you can have in the account. You contribute funds from your taxed income; the initial investment has no tax break. However, from that point, the funds in the ISA are 'invisible' to the Inland Revenue. You will never pay tax on the capital growth or income from an ISA, so you can take a significant tax-free income if you wish at any time. You will never need to fill anything in on your tax form, either.

If you have a higher income, you might also consider Venture Capital Trusts and the Enterprise Investment Scheme as ways of getting an immediate tax break if you're in the UK. VCTs also offer freedom from income tax on dividends and capital gains in the future. However, these are higher-risk investments and should not represent more than 10-15% of your portfolio, if that much.

In the US, the Roth IRA offers you some extra flexibility, together with helpful tax breaks. You can take out your contributions at any time, but you can only take out your earnings once you're fifty-nine and a half without paying a 10% early withdrawal penalty.

Municipal bonds are not in themselves great investments, but they pay tax-free interest. If you are in the highest tax bracket, this can make them quite attractive; as they are tax-free, you are getting a higher net yield, even though the gross yield declared looks unappetizing; however, you need to do the numbers on this as the math is all-important.

Once you've reached your Roth IRA limits, further equity investment must be held in a regular brokerage account, either in stocks or in index funds. Index funds are a way to increase the risk profile into areas such as private equity, emerging markets, or early-stage tech stocks without having to make bets on individual companies, so they're beneficial for FIRE investors.

Remember to take advantage of any 'free' money you get from your employer, for instance, employer contributions to a pension or a 401k. Even if your 'regular' pension is not your priority investment, it's worth keeping contributions up to the threshold for getting your 'free' money.

Finally, real estate makes a compelling investment for FIRE portfolios, not as a source of capital gains but as a source of recurring income. Building up a portfolio of rental-producing investments can help diversify your income and protect you from down years in the stock market (garages, lock-ups and parking spaces can offer a cheaper entry point than residential properties, though you should be an expert on the area before investing).

So, *should* you retire early?

FIRE assumes that early retirement is a no-brainer. But is it?

For some, it certainly can be. If you're in a highly paid career but one where burnout is common (for instance, finance or law) or where promotion opportunities start to close down markedly once you get past a certain age, adopting FIRE will give you the flexibility to switch career tracks, for instance. Suppose you want to move into consulting or entrepreneurship. In that case, FIRE will let you do so without running the risk of bankruptcy.

But there are disadvantages to following the FIRE program. If you make huge lifestyle sacrifices in your twenties and thirties to save money, you could miss out on experiences such as travel and doing fun things with friends.

Some early retirees find other people don't know how to relate to them. The only forty-year-olds who don't have jobs are usually the unemployed. Without a job title, what's your status? Are you C-suite, management, or blue-collar? If you got a lot of status from your job, you may feel lost without it. If your job delivered a lot of the stimulation in your life, and most of your friends were colleagues, you may end up bored or lonely. You'll also find that if, after a couple of years, you think you've made a mistake, or your money isn't covering as good a lifestyle as you thought it would, returning to work in your late forties or fifties could be difficult. And just as happens with normal retirement, you may find that once you have lots of free time, you somehow end up spending lots of money, even if it's only on Starbucks.

Some people prefer to be 'normal.' After all, it's so much easier to follow a track that's laid out for you.

You'll also need to make your retirement savings last much longer. If you retire at forty, you'll likely need to cover more than forty and maybe fifty years' retirement. You'll need to cover nearly twenty years out of your investments before you get anything out of pension funds and longer than that before the state starts paying you.

Inflation and volatile markets could knock your investments, and you may find you've underestimated the cost of care.

Having a backup plan is sensible, given the multiple uncertainties.

Don't rely on a single source of income. This is why having both real estate and stocks is useful; your tenants will probably continue paying rent even if your stocks fall and some of the companies you hold cut their dividends. If you have an additional source of income, such as a 'hobby' business or a monetized blog or video channel, even better.

Have an emergency fund as well as your investments. If markets are tanking, you don't want to start selling stock at low valuations to fund your lifestyle; take it out of the emergency fund. Basically, you're writing yourself a check, and you can pay it back later.

Is FIRE for everybody?

FIRE has come under some criticism for being exclusive. In particular, Silicon Valley-based FIRE forums can be 'too white' and 'too male,' with most of their members being highly paid programmers and developers with no kids. Suppose you're a Harvard graduate with a huge bonus. In that case, you can afford to put 70% of your salary straight into stocks and don't need to sweat it on cutting out cappuccinos.

However, women and particularly Black women, have started flocking to FIRE and setting up their own blogs to encourage others. For many of these FIRE advocates, it's not about retiring at thirty but about avoiding the money worries that their parents had or ensuring they have more choices in their lives. Their 'retire early' may not be in their thirties but at, say, fifty-two, or it may let them change career in their forties.

Traditional FIRE also didn't really build in much thought about having children and the financial burden that can create. Sam Dogen, known to many as the 'Financial Samurai,' retired at thirty-four, but he's gone back to work now he has children because he wants to be able to pay their college tuition.

Lean FIRE with kids would be tough love indeed; no music lessons, no extra sports, no treats, no school trips or summer camp. In fact, if you read books written by people who were brought up in cults, you can see that such an extreme really equals 'no childhood.' Increasing your earnings by working extensive overtime or running a side hustle might also mean you'd miss out on your kids' childhood, so you may need to make choices. However, you could aim to do as much as possible to keep contributing to your investments while prioritizing your children.

It will also be interesting talking through your financial choices with your children once they're old enough. They may see the point in adopting FIRE for themselves once they grow up!

Ultimately, whether or not you adopt FIRE will be a personal choice. But there's a lot to be learned from the program, whatever your final decision: financial discipline, mindful spending, regular saving. And even if you start with FIRE and sideline it when children arrive, you'll at least have a good financial base for starting your family!

Chapter Nine
PASSIVE INCOME

"Some people want it to happen, some wish it would happen, others make it happen" – Michael Jordan

What is passive income?

Passive income is a stream of income that continues without your participation. You may have made an initial investment, such as buying shares that pay you a dividend, or you may have created a side hustle that pays you royalties or advertising fees without you doing more work. The whole idea is that instead of 'work for hire,' you're working to create an asset.

You could build a house, but nowadays it's more likely that you've built a website, a series of online training courses, or an Android app. The idea is not 'get rich quick,' but rather to build something that will keep delivering an income over the years.

Some passive income requires a small investment of time. For instance, if you rent a room out on AirBNB, you'll need to welcome guests and change the bedclothes and towels, but that's not much work, and you could even outsource it if you're renting out a separate flat. In the same way, an author gets royalties on books they have published, maybe years before, but they may want to do some press publicity or bookshop signings or go to a literary festival or Comic-Con every so often to keep sales flowing. Nonetheless, they don't *have* to do anything; if the book sells, they'll get their royalties.

If you have built passive income over the years coming up to your retirement, you'll have an extra income stream to add to your other investments and pensions.

Broadly, there are three main ways to build passive income. The first is investing. Dividend investing and buying bonds are good ways of creating passive income, but I think I've already written about those kinds of investment in enough detail in previous chapters. Second, you can build assets, such as a website or a series of DIY-project books. Third, you can share assets you already have, for instance by AirBNBing a room in your home, or lending out kit that you already own.

Here are just a few ideas of how to build passive income:

- Publish books on Kindle or Smashwords.
- Create journals and record books on Kindle Createspace.
- Create a training course on Udemy, SkillShare or Coursera.
- Build a website on a topic you find fascinating and use it to build affiliate income and pay-per-click advertising.
- Sell your photos online.
- Create an app that does something useful (or entertaining).
- Rent out your parking space.
- Create a blog or YouTube channel.
- Rent out kit like lawnmowers, tools, camp tents, scaffolding, or marquees.
- Sell your designs online through sites like CafePress or Zazzle.

Things you might need to think about

Side hustles aren't just for those on low incomes. Some very high-flying professionals also have side hustles, for instance with AirBNB apartments or writing erotica.

You'd be surprised to find out some people actually had a day job! Senior civil servant Phyllis White was better known as PD James, the detective novelist, and carried on working in government service till she retired. Part-time poet TS Eliot, on the other hand, gave up his job as a banker when he was offered a directorship with publishers Faber & Faber. And famously, composer Philip Glass worked as a taxi driver, removals man, and plumber – even while he was writing his operas!

If you love your job, but it isn't quite generating enough income for you to enjoy life properly, then think about creating some passive income so that you're not relying just on your job to pay the bills. Of course, other great things about passive income are that you can't be sacked from it and there is no boss to satisfy; you are the boss.

However, only a few people manage to get their side hustles off the ground. Lots of people have great ideas, but they get bogged down. Perhaps they don't have enough time, or they don't have enough money, or they don't have enough experience. I have met people who 'invented' the RV, Starbucks, online degrees, but they didn't actually do anything with the idea.

So rather than trying to come up with ideas from scratch, first of all, sit down and think what skills, abilities, assets or knowledge you have – or can easily obtain – to create a passive income business.

Then you need to brainstorm. Remember, even if your skill is one that's usually used as 'work for hire,' you might have a way of turning it into passive income. For instance, if you're a painter and decorator, a website showing 'paint disasters and how to avoid them' or a YouTube channel providing really good instructions on just how to achieve a spotless finish might be a good way to start. What about an app that tells people exactly how much paint they'll need for a job? If you have a friend who's a software developer, why don't you see if you can work on that together?

Writing books, blogs, creating podcasts or videos on a subject you care about can really work well. For instance, train spotting, bird watching, girl scouting, updating furniture, and even renovating a French château have all made great side hustles and sources of passive income for YouTubers and bloggers.

Brainstorming, either on your own or with friends and family, can help create more ideas. To start with, don't rule anything out, even if it looks pretty stupid. Just concentrate on getting as many ideas as possible. Then look at what you have, think about whether there's a market for each idea and whether you have the skills or assets needed to develop it. If you need a new skill, put that idea away for the moment – it's going to take you time to develop that skill, unless you can subcontract it.

Join groups for entrepreneurs and attend networking events; these are great ways to get new ideas.

Find an idea that you can execute right now, and just do it. It might sink without trace. Get whatever feedback you can, for instance from reviews. You may just need to change one or two small things, or you may just need a bit more marketing. On the other hand, if it simply didn't work, you still have that list of ideas, so get on to the next one. Go for the win, don't procrastinate, get active, and you should, given a couple of tries, come up with something that is producing a little income.

At that point you have two options. One is to do some more marketing to get more income out of what you have already. The other is to get another idea up and running and create a little portfolio of side hustles. In fact, you probably already spotted the fact that you could do both!

Ideas for passive income

Real estate

There are so many different ways you can make money from real estate. And there are so many different kinds of real estate you can make money from. So it's important to choose the business model that fits you and your pocketbook.

If you have a limited pocketbook, start with crowdfunding. Property crowdfunding is a great way to build passive income. We already discussed that in the chapter on investments.

Buy and hold

If you can buy property and hold it in the long term, you will get rental income. How much work you put in depends on whether you manage the property actively or hire a manager. For instance, a friend has six apartments in a townhouse, and pays $150 a month for the whole complex to be managed for him (yes, that's a bargain; a college friend does the management). The regular income is one of the reasons this is one of the commonest investment strategies for retirees.

The entry ticket can be quite high. However, you may be able to get finance if you can put down 20% of the price as a deposit and can demonstrate that the rent will cover your finance costs. You'll likely pay a higher rate of interest than on a home loan, though. In the UK, buy-to-let mortgages require you to put a 25% deposit down. Typically, rents go up with inflation, so this is a good protection for your purchasing power.

The buy-and-hold real estate strategy is a common investment option, since it promises both long-term gains and short-term cash flow. Rental income from the property generates short-term cash that you can use to pay off your loan and put cash in your bank account. Over time, the loan will be paid down and the property value will appreciate, boosting your net asset value. That allows you to profit when you are ready to sell the property down the line. Alternatively, you could use your accumulated rental surplus to build a down-payment for a second property.

(Some people invest in properties which generate a rental income *lower* than the debt servicing payment. That's very unwise; you'll only get any return at all if the property increases markedly in value. In fact, when a lot of people are buying on this basis, it's usually a sign that the market is overvalued).

Read the press to find out where you will get the best returns. Some cities offer very high returns but have poor demographics (e.g., a declining population with high unemployment), so you should avoid those. Look for cities where city government is spending on rehabilitation or on new transport links and infrastructure, where employment is strong and real estate prices may not have risen to reflect the fact. In the US, Albuquerque, Atlanta, Baltimore, Chicago, Dallas, Dayton, Orlando, Pittsburgh and Huntsville, for example, all get quoted right now as interesting markets for just these reasons. You can also use Zillow and AirBNB to assess property prices and likely rental returns.

For cities, check public transportation access. Being close to a subway station can pay off. If new lines are being built, that can improve your rental levels once they come in; obviously, the time to buy is before they start operating! Don't forget to check out how high local property taxes are. You may also want to check out the school districts (but not if you're buying studio flats), coffee shops, parks, trails and other amenities. Remember to define who your renter is likely to be. If you're buying large family houses, local nightclubs are probably less important than schools. Remember, too, that universities and large hospitals, particularly teaching hospitals, can be great sources of customers, since they often have staff staying a year or two, for whom buying a home isn't an option.

If you're buying away from home, don't be the innocent fall-guy. Do your homework. Real estate agents, builders and property managers may try to take advantage of the fact you're not from their city to sell you the property that has been longest on their books, charge you above the going rate, and make promises that anyone in town knows are unrealistic. And if you're going to manage your own property, make sure you have a list of good contractors (or that you are one – having DIY skills can really pay off), and make sure you know the law applying to landlords and tenants. Slip-ups can be very costly.

You'll also want a good accountant. There are various tax breaks available to landlords in the US, such as setting your income against any loan you used to buy or refurbish the property, and there are various different tax treatments you can choose. In the UK, the tax treatment of rental properties has been significantly tightened up, but a good accountant will save you meaningful sums all the same.

Flipping isn't passive income, but some investors do very well by adopting a **flip-and-hold** strategy. They buy property that needs a light refurb, getting a discount on the market price, so their long-term return is higher. Once they have rented the property out, they refinance it and, when they find the right opportunity, they'll do another flip. That can add 2-3% to your gross yield, so it's a great strategy if you have what it takes to make it work.

You might also buy properties from foreclosure but be very careful if you do – it's a rather specialized market and has some significant pitfalls. Wall Street firms buying distressed properties aim for a 5-7% return; as an individual investor you should probably aim for 10%, which gives you a larger margin of error.

Do remember to take account of maintenance and repair needs. You won't get to keep all the rental payments, as occasionally you will need to fix a boiler or toilet, waterproof the roof, give the woodwork a fresh coat of paint or just refresh a property in between tenants. 1% a year at the very least should go into a 'sinking fund' so you have repair money available.

One good way to think about buy-and-hold real estate is how many properties you need to reach your goals. For instance, suppose my goal is $60,000 a year. If the average property where I invest has rental levels of $750 a month, that's $9,000 a year before costs. So I will need seven properties to get there (if one or two of your properties are particularly well specified and get above market rent, you might only need six).

House hacking / renting out a room

If you're not able to buy a rental property, you may be able to rent out part of your home. That might just involve letting out a spare bedroom; in the UK you can earn up to £7,500 from this before you pay any tax. You might rent out your garage, barn space, or parking area.

You won't get rich doing this, but it can help to pay down your home loan faster and even free up some money for investment.

If you think about the potential for house hacking before you buy, you might keep your eyes open for properties that lend themselves to this treatment. We'll talk about that in the next section.

Short-term letting

Letting through AirBNB is potentially much more lucrative than long-term letting. However, that comes with a number of caveats. First – assuming you're buying a property to let out, rather than letting out a spare room in your own home – it's much more labor intensive. You'll have to do the cleaning, change the sheets, ensure people have keys (or use a keycode), and so on. Nowadays there are companies in many AirBNB hotspots which can do this for you, but of course you'll be paying for it. You'll also be paying the utility bills.

Some cities have also introduced restrictions on short-term letting. Miami and Santa Monica have some tight regulations, while New York and San Francisco allow limited rentals to hosts who are full-time residents. Make sure you know about the regulations and about any proposed regulations, before you invest.

One cute way to AirBNB might be a form of house hacking: buy a duplex or a house with a guest house or chalet in the garden and rent out your extra space. You might even be able to make what's called a 'sneaky duplex' if your floor plan is right, just by knocking through an exterior door to one of your downstairs rooms, making it into a suite (it needs a bathroom, but for AirBNB, it *doesn't* need a kitchen, just a microwave, some cups, plates, wine glasses or tumblers, crockery, and a fridge).

Real estate shares

These are another good way to build passive income and are great for the everyday American. REITs yield more than the S&P 500 and some good-quality REITs deliver yields between 4% and 8%, as well as giving you capital growth over the long term. Like property crowdfunding, they give you the opportunity to invest in big-ticket sectors like logistics, apartment buildings, offices, or malls, which aren't available to individual investors. You can even invest in cell towers, data centers, prisons, self-store units, timberland or farmland (MREITs, which don't invest in property but lend to property investors and developers, also exist, but they are in the minority).

REITs have a tax advantage. Normally, a company makes a profit, pays tax on the profit, then it pays you some of the profit as a dividend. A REIT, on the other hand, commits to pay out at least 90% of its taxable income as dividends; in return for that, it doesn't pay tax on its income, which is passed straight through to you. So that income only gets taxed once, when you pay tax on it. REITs work the same in the UK and US, with a few differences; there are international REITs in other countries, too.

REITs are huge. In the US, they collectively own over $4.5 trn worth of real estate, out of which $3 trn is held by public REITs (holding 535,000 or so different properties). Stock-market-listed REITs are worth more than $1.5 trn.

Private and non-listed REITs exist but may not be suitable for most investors. Stock-market-listed REITs are just as easy as any other stock to buy and sell through a broker and have to make SEC filings showing their financial position every quarter. Historically, they have delivered competitive total returns; they are also good diversification investments, since they have comparatively low correlation with stocks and bonds.

Buying REITs via an ETF is possible and offers a simple way to gain exposure to the sector, both domestically and internationally. However, this won't necessarily give you the best income return. If your main concern is to build income, you'll want to analyze your own portfolio. Get a mentor or sit down and get to grips with the detailed methods of analyzing cap rates (the percentage rate by which you can multiply rental income to arrive at the price of a property; it's basically just the reverse calculation from working out a yield) and funds from operations (FFO – the basic cash flow figure, adding back depreciation on the property portfolio and subtracting any capital gains on the sale of holdings).

Don't just buy on the dividend yield. Make sure the REIT doesn't have too much debt, or tenants who aren't paying rent (often, the REITs which have the highest stated yields are those which are financially stressed, making it likely that the dividend will be cut). For instance, several healthcare REITS in the US (such as Omega Healthcare Investors, Medical Properties Trust) have had non-paying tenants after Covid affected the skilled nursing home sector. They have high yields but a lot of risk.

What are the big benefits of REITs compared to direct investment? You don't have to manage the properties – "tenants, toilets and trash" as the saying goes – and you don't have to pay legal fees on acquiring the properties, either. Also, you can build a holding just buying $100 or £100 or so of shares every month – this is a good low-ticket entry point to real estate.

By the way, some REITs will actually pay you every month! Here's a list of some of the main contenders:

Company	**Ticker Symbol**
SL Green Realty	SLG
EPR Properties	EPR
STAG Industrial	STAG
Realty Income	O
Agree Realty	ADC
Gladstone Land	LAND

Company	Ticker Symbol
LTC Properties	LTC

(If you're not used to ticker symbols, they're the short way of referring to the stock. And it's much easier if you're trading ETFs, for example, to remember a ticker symbol like VNQ or SELD than the full name of the ETF. Some are quite fun: Franklin Resources, Inc. has BEN and Asia Tigers Fund has GRR).

If you don't want to become a specialist on REITs and pore through their financial figures, then you can invest in a REIT ETF. The gorilla in this space is Vanguard Real Estate (VNQ) with $36 bn assets under management and an annual expense charge of just 0.12%. iShares Core US REIT ETF (USRT) is similar, but does not, unlike Vanguard, invest in real estate development or service companies. Vanguard also offers a purely international (i.e., no US exposure) REIT ETF, VNQI, tracking more than 600 international REITs from thirty different countries.

There are other options. Income investors might be tempted by the Global X Super Dividend REIT ETF (SRET), which distributes income every month and currently yields over 7%, but its expense ratio of 0.58% is quite a bit higher that the other ETFs mentioned.

Don't confuse REIGs with REITs. A Real Estate Investment Group is a business that focuses on real estate. It might buy, develop, or sell properties, finance property, flip properties, buy land for subdivision into lots, or apartment buildings to sell off the apartments separately. They can also manage properties for other landlords. A REIG's activities aren't limited to property, as a REIT's are.

The advantage of buying into a REIG is that you can access development and management returns, not just rental returns as with most REITs. Some REIGs get involved in house flipping, as well as rentals.

Sometimes they are set up by real estate companies to buy large, multi-family buildings, administering and managing the property, and offering units as a passive investment for smaller investors. Naturally, the fund will charge for the management of the property. Other times, groups of larger investors will get together to invest their funds and knowledge in a portfolio of properties, and will sell units to smaller investors to help finance the investments.

REIGs can be structured in many different ways, including as part of a real estate crowdfunding. However, they have a few downsides compared to REITs: they may have a higher entry ticket and may have costly fees. Also, they may be less liquid - you may not be able to sell your stake easily, or at all.

Online education

This is growing fast. Ninety-two million new learners registered on Coursera in 2021, up from twenty-one million in 2016. Those learners are all over the world, with 13.6m in India, 2.4m in Russia, 3.3m in China, and 1.6m in Egypt, as well as seventeen million in the US. The pandemic really drove use of online education, both from people who wanted to learn a new skill during lockdown and from employers who needed to be able to deliver training without being able to get their staff together physically.

If you've thought of some good ideas but don't have the right skills to make use of them – for instance, you need to learn video editing or basic programming – online education can be a big help. Many courses are free.

But the really huge opportunity, of course, is for you to teach your skills online. Choose something you have real experience in; it doesn't have to be from your career or academic knowledge. Francis Bourgeois has become huge on TikTok with his videos about trainspotting. He's a real expert but he also brings a gentle, wistful humor to his videos. You might be able to teach a language. For instance, there are some really good teaching videos on YouTube if you want to learn 'how French people really speak French,' setting you straight on idioms and slang as well as more formal grammar and vocabulary. If you happen to have a bilingual home background, fantastic!

Try to find something specific that differentiates you. There are lots and lots of guitar teachers around, but 'Play the top ten licks and riffs with me' or 'Why is Jimi Hendrix so good?' would be really specific courses that could resonate with a lot of people (an Australian university actually offered a module on Bohemian Rhapsody, looking at it in real detail. That was huge fun but delivered some unexpected learning points, too). Also think about how you could add more content later.

As you progress in your career, you might want to offer specialized teaching on technical or theoretical concepts, or you could offer advice on soft skills. I wish I had been able to access human resources managers' advice on how to present myself at interviews when I got started. Now, I can, thanks to online education.

Equally, you might have acquired knowledge about investment, real estate, or entrepreneurship as you developed your passive income. That too can be shared.

As well as generating passive income from video courses and books, you might also want to consider teaching personally online to boost your income. On average, you could earn $19 an hour before tax, teaching online. In many areas, you won't need a qualification (though you ought to check). Of course, if you are a retired teacher, there is nothing to stop you carrying on in a private capacity as a tutor for anything you used to teach; you'll have loads of skills and experience gained over the years.

You'll need to search for the best platforms. Skillshare, Udemy, or Teachable, for instance, allow you to monetize your courses. YouTube also has potential for building an audience, which you can then monetize if your channel is successful. You'll want to have some blogging or social media presence to generate leads, and put some effort into marketing your product, for instance using affiliate marketing. You could earn up to around $5,000 a month if you're successful.

For the best results, try to find a mentor, and review other courses to see how they are presented. What do you like about the presentation? What don't you like about it? How can you do better? It's a crowded market, but if you come up with the right product and a clear brand, you can still do well.

Online platforms can help you create content and manage your payments. Platforms you might consider when you're starting out include:

- Teachable is an easy-to-use, hosted platform that will help you create and market your content. But it costs $29 a month as well as a 5% transaction fee.
- Skillshare has a big following and great marketing, and there's no cost to publish a class, but you'll need to fit their format (forty minutes plus a class project).
- MemberPress is part of WordPress, a very well-known website design tool. For $179.50 a year, you'll get a visual course builder, powerful membership features, scheduling and email marketing tools. It supports multiple payment systems and takes no percentage on your sales.
- LearnDash, another WordPress-based tool, has a drag-and-drop course builder and adds gamification and sales funnels for your course. Prices start from $199 a year.
- Thinkific is fully hosted, very easy to use and free (in a limited version). If you want to try out a couple of ideas without spending a lot, it's a great way to get started.
- Udemy is also free, but it only pays a 37% royalty on sales. With nearly fifty million students, it gives you access to a captive customer base, and that's a big advantage when you're starting out.

With online teaching, you decide when to work, in your own time. But if you build a training course, it can make money while you fish, shop, sleep or hike – and you can also advertise extra on-line coaching via the course. Once they've done the course, people will regard you as an authority in your field, so your sales pitch is already done.

Become an author

This is a great way to create passive, long-term royalty income. Again, take stock of what you know that will interest other people. Can you write a book that helps others with their problems? Giving up smoking, getting out of debt, and getting fit are all issues that a lot of people want help with, and if you've been through the process yourself, you may be able to do that. Or can you help people get more out of their leisure time? Perhaps you can help readers improve their photographs, make their gardens more beautiful or productive, or start journaling or painting.

Eight percent of Americans read more than fifty books a year; another 20% read more than ten, and another 40% read at least one. So that's a pretty big market out there. It's easy to access via Amazon's Kindle program, which allows you to self-publish. If you find it difficult to write, you might find it useful to just sit down with a sound recorder on and talk about the subject; you can get it down in print later.

There are a number of courses available on self-publishing. There are also plenty of freelances who can help you, for instance with designing a book cover or by editing your manuscript before you make it into an eBook. Once you've written your book, you could have an income for life. But it's best to keep going – your first book might not be a best-seller, but if you keep putting out new books on the topic, you will gradually build up a solid catalog. That's what we call 'long-tail' income, and just like investment, it will often snowball.

There's also a market for low-content books – that is, books which give the user a format for their own records, such as diaries, music practice books, planners, and perhaps coloring books. You can use Amazon to offer these without having to print and stock the books, and they can do very well if you have an interesting idea or just a cute cat on the cover.

Affiliate marketing

Affiliate marketing is another way to make a stream of passive income. If you direct customers to a company's website, either to generate traffic or to sell particular items, you'll get a commission fee which comes out of that company's advertising budget. It's a way for the company to broaden its reach. For instance, if you are a military history buff and run a YouTube channel visiting battlefields and forts, you might have a page showing the best books to buy on certain topics and directing customers to Amazon; each time someone buys one of those books, you'll get a commission.

I'd suggest affiliate marketing isn't something you want to target as your first passive income idea. You need to have already established a loyal audience for it to work. But if you have a blog or podcast or YouTube channel or website, it can make good sense. Make sure you only get involved with quality affiliates though. If a business strategy website started up an affiliate marketing deal with a Bitcoin exchange, for instance, that might make many of its users question the quality of the content they're reading. Equally, I always have an uneasy feeling when I see a serious newspaper or journal displaying clickbait style celebrity stories at the bottom of the page.

There are three types of affiliate marketing:

1. **Unattached** – you have no connection at all to the product or service being promoted, other than the fact you're promoting it.
2. **Related** – you have a relationship with the product or service; for instance, you review cosmetics and you have a link to a beauty products store, but you don't give advice about the particular products.
3. **Involved** – this is a deeper connection; it's where you have used the product or service and believe others will have the same positive experience. If you review cosmetics *and* you think Glamazon Beauty has absolutely the best products, and you're willing to recommend them, this is involved affiliate marketing.

You'll probably get better returns from related or involved marketing. You may get commissions amounting to 5-10% of the sales price of the products, which can amount to a tidy monthly income if you get things right.

Multi-level marketing (MLM)

This can produce a good passive income stream after you've put some effort into it, but you need to be careful to check out the business. Some are not much more than pyramid schemes. However, long-standing schemes like Avon, Herbalife, Primerica and Amway are reputable and proven to be profitable.

MLM is a way for a company to organize its direct sales. You become a distributor of the product, but you can also sign up new distributors and bring them into the business; you'll then get a commission on their sales as well as yours.

While initially, you'll need to put effort into selling, networking, and expanding your business, once you have a number of recruits, you can step back a little and let them do the work. You'll still get an income. So hard work at the start can pay off later. It's not completely passive income, as you'll probably still want to do some motivational work with your recruits and make sure they're signing up new recruits in their turn, but the larger your business gets, the less you'll need to do!

Debt investment

This might be an option. Basically, you lend money to a firm, and you get it back with interest. It can be secured on assets, for instance if you're lending money to a real estate developer, or it can be unsecured, in which case you'll need to rely on an assessment of the borrower's creditworthiness.

The returns from debt investing are not all that high compared to the risk if you do it yourself, particularly if you're lending to smaller businesses. If you want to help out a small business that you know, and you think it's going to grow, you'll get better returns if you take equity in the business. My advice would be that you are better sticking to crowdfunding through a reputable platform or investing in bonds as part of your portfolio.

Before we move onto the next chapter, I want to make a book recommendation with a promise that you will read it, if you haven't already.

The book is called 'The 4-Hour Work Week' by Tim Ferriss. Not only will he inspire you to work less for more money, he will give you some great ideas on how to do this. It definitely inspired me along the way.

Chapter Ten
SMART RETIREMENT INVESTMENTS

So far, everything in this book has applied to anyone, however much they earn or possess. This chapter is for those of you who have a little more money and want to preserve, and indeed increase, your capital, and (if possible) shelter it from tax, too. You'll probably find that quite a few of these opportunities are only available to high-net-worth investors (which the SEC defines as having at least $1.5m net assets, or $750,000 in liquid assets such as stocks and cash).

Angel investing

An 'angel' invests their own money in a small or start-up business in return for a stake in the business, usually between 10% and 25%. Most angel investors aren't just wealthy, they also have a good background in business, either as investors, or as high-level executives or entrepreneurs. That gives them good instincts as well as the ability to conduct proper due diligence on the prospects they're looking at.

Angel investing is higher risk than most other forms of investing. Remember that a high percentage of start-ups don't make it to their fifth birthday. It's also quite long term; you may have to wait five years or more to get any reward. You'll probably want to stick to areas you know something about; tech can deliver great rewards, but if your background is in retailing and e-commerce, you might be better off leaving the fintechs and blockchain companies alone.

You'll also want to make sure you take professional advice, not just on the investment but also on the documentation and the precise structuring of the deal. Ideally, you should also bring something to the party; for instance, you might be able to introduce the team to potential partners or customers or help structure their finances. Angel investors usually work quite closely with their teams. This isn't like stock exchange investing, at arm's length (if you've ever watched Dragon's Den or Shark Tank, you'll see how the investors explain what they can offer to the entrepreneur making the pitch, in addition to their investment).

Angel investors represent a real lifeline for many small businesses which are too small or too young for most banks to be interested. The upside can be considerable if the business is a success. If you invest in a business which eventually lists its shares on the stock exchange through an Initial Public Offering, you could make 10,000% to 100,000% on your initial seed investment!

However, many of these companies do not succeed, so most angels prefer to spread their money across a number of opportunities, so they have a diversified portfolio.

You may also be able to get tax credits on your investment. For instance, the states of Iowa and Minnesota offer Angel Investment Tax Credits; in the UK, the Enterprise Investment Scheme (EIS) and Seed Enterprise Investment Scheme (SEIS) give tax relief to investors who buy a stake in qualifying businesses. The SEIS is targeted at start-ups and smaller companies, while the EIS targets companies that are at a slightly later stage; some finance houses, like Mercia, offer EIS funds.

It's worth doing some networking before you start out, and perhaps joining an angel investing syndicate or club. That can also help you diversify your holdings. Whatever you do, remember that you really shouldn't be investing more than 10% of your portfolio, at the very most, in these opportunities, however tempting they may look.

EIS	SEIS
Up to seven years trading history	Fewer than two years trading history
Up to 250 employees	Up to twenty-five employees
You can invest up to £1m per tax year	You can invest up to £100,000 per tax year

Seed funding

Seed funding is angel investing on steroids – it's pure start-up funding, so all you're buying is a stake in a business plan. Often, it will only cover the funds needed to produce a prototype, or proof of concept, or feasibility study; if that fails, there won't be a business to invest in. If it works, the business will need more funding, and you'll either have to stump up, or see your stake diluted. So this is really high-octane, high-risk stuff.

I'd suggest you only get involved in seed funding if you already have a track record in angel investing *and* have good contacts, such as angels you have invested with previously.

Public equity

This is just another name for good old-fashioned stocks and shares. A private company may have a very small number of shareholders, and the requirements to produce financial filings are quite limited, making it difficult for investors to get information unless they have strong links with the company. A public company lists its shares on a stock exchange; usually, companies which have been privately funded will at some point have an Initial Public Offering (IPO), selling newly created shares to the open market.

A public company needs to produce a prospectus with detailed information on the business, and quarterly financial reports. It's usually also a requirement that there is a certain number of shareholders to enable trading to be facilitated. Therefore, you have better liquidity than with a private company. You can sell fairly simply through a broker, whereas with a private company, you may not be able to sell, and in fact you might even be subject to a lock-in clause preventing you from selling until a certain amount of time has passed.

The entry ticket is also much lower. You can become a stock market tycoon on $10 a week if you invest well and keep investing; the entry ticket for most private companies is going to be $10,000 to $25,000, if not even more.

Entrepreneurship

I already talked a bit about side hustles and creating passive income, but you might want to go the whole way to starting your own full-time business. However, entrepreneurship is high risk: up to 90% of start-ups fail within the first few years. You'll need passion, and you'll need to make real effort, if you want to succeed.

That said, you can mitigate the risks by starting small, in some cases. For instance, you might start with a food truck rather than take on a restaurant lease. You can then develop your menu, style, and customer base, and decide, when you have loyal customers, whether to move into restaurant premises, or perhaps buy a second truck and take on staff. You can also minimize risk by outsourcing some of your business functions to freelancers, rather than taking on permanent staff.

An entrepreneur can be defined as someone who starts and manages a new business, taking personal and financial risk. They might be small business owners, content creators or founders of a start-up tech business.

They might operate as sole traders or incorporate their business (which has advantages in limiting any liabilities).

While entrepreneurship sounds like fun, it's actually grindingly daunting. Your workload will be high, and it could take years to build up the business. When you're creating side hustles, you can move on from project to project, and if one fails, well, you've still got a day job. When you're a full-time entrepreneur, you're going to have to stick at it. And sometimes, it will be really hard to do.

You don't just have to find an idea; it has to be a profitable one. You then have to develop and differentiate your product or service. You'll need to validate your product by getting testimonials or by getting a prototype made. You'll need to write a business plan and secure funding. And then you'll need to find customers – whether you have one major customer at the outset (which might work well for a software business, for instance), or many retail customers. You'll need to be able to do everything: operations, finance, marketing, sales. It's a big ask.

You might just decide to go freelance at what you already do. This can work well if you're being held back in your current job. For instance, if you are an advertising buyer, if you can help people develop their online businesses, you may do better and have a more enjoyable life if you set up your own agency. All kinds of services can be offered as a freelance: translation, software, cyber security, games development, website creation, songwriting, voice-overs, video making, article or blog writing, or consultancy. One of my friends is a marine engineering consultant; at fifty, he decided he was tired of working for a multinational, so he started his own business, which pays just as well but is half as much work!

However, if you want to develop beyond just being a solo freelancer, you'll need to think about how to expand or how to create scalable services. For instance, if you're in advertising, you could go the traditional route and create an agency, or you could try to develop a generic service that can be automated and sold as a standardized package, or even on a software as a service (SAAS) basis.

Interim management is something that can suit senior executives who want a new challenge. Companies often hit the skids or find that they don't know how to grow; sometimes family companies find this out when they're looking at their succession plans. An interim manager can go in, assess the problems, and take action - sometimes quite drastic action - aiming to get the company set on course within six months or so. This is very well remunerated if you're good at it.

You could also build up a retail business, becoming a drop-shipper on eBay or Amazon, or creating your own branded products for sale on Amazon. FBA (Fulfilled By Amazon) is a good way to get started; you don't need to take delivery of the goods, as you can get them sent direct to Amazon, who will take care of the shipping process. However, this has become gradually more competitive over the last few years. It's not a get-rich-quick scheme, but you can build a business - and you can even sell that business to a consolidator once it's become successful.

Of course, if you have a couple of great side hustles, you can decide to go full time with them. That, again, minimizes the risk you're taking, because you are already successful at what you're doing.

Chapter Eleven
PLANNING FOR LONG-TERM CARE

Long-term care needs often get overlooked in retirement planning. Even when people think about medical care, they often think about needing a surgical operation, being in hospital for a week or so, or end-of-life care. But in fact, most people who need long-term care just need help with daily life, sometimes because of mental inability (such as Parkinson's disease or dementia), and sometimes because of frailty or partial disablement (for instance from osteo-arthritis or a stroke).

If you have a family history of any of these conditions, you might want to devote particular attention to the possible need for long-term care later in life. Roughly half of all retirees need long-term care at some point.

How much would it cost?

You may be lucky enough to have family who live nearby and can help you with your daily life. However, don't assume that they will be able or willing to spend a large part of their lives looking after you. It can be a full-time job, and if they already have a job and have children, there may not be much spare capacity.

US

A 2016 brief from the Assistant Secretary for Planning and Evaluation (ASPE) showed that 11% of Americans could end up paying over $100,000 for long-term care, while an unfortunate 15% might pay over $250,000. These costs can vary substantially depending on a number of factors. For instance, you could choose a shared room in a nursing home, but that's not even considered a possibility by some people. You could choose a rather basic facility or a more upscale facility, or you could choose in-home care. Costs also depend on location. Alaska and Hawaii are pricy, as are the Northeast and the West Coast, but if you live somewhere in the Midwest, you'll be paying less.

Another thing you might think about is whether curtailment of other costs will leave spare income. For instance, if you spent three months or more of every year traveling, that's a big slice of income that went for tickets and hotels but is now available to fund care instead.

Of course, you might be one of the lucky half (actually 48%) of the US population who don't need long-term care. So while you want to think about it, you don't necessarily want to plan for it to happen. But you do need to think about where the money would come from if it were needed.

- If you need residential long-term care, you may no longer need your home. You could sell it and use the equity to pay for care.
- An income annuity can be planned to cover your care costs. That's not what they're designed for, specifically, but it's a good way to ensure you don't run out of money.
- A long-term care insurance policy will pay for some costs but isn't always as good a solution as it looks; there may be a waiting period or maximum payout and getting a new policy once you've retired can be difficult.
- Medicaid will cover long-term care, but only once you have already exhausted your own ability to pay. It only helps 34% of Americans who need long-term care.

- Some annuities have a 'living benefit rider,' which will increase your income if you need long-term care. However, your beneficiaries will get a reduced death benefit when you are gone.
- Some universal life insurance plans will advance the death benefit in monthly payments if you need universal care.

UK

The situation in the UK is a bit different. Some financial help is available from local councils and from the NHS, but the care system is complex and eligibility depends on the reason for the need for long-term care.

If your needs are mainly due to a health condition, the NHS may pay for your care under NHS CHC (Continuing Health Care). In this case, your care will be free. This doesn't depend on the health condition you have, but on the type of care you need. If it exceeds what a council can offer, because of the severity of the condition, the complexity of your needs, or an unpredictable condition which needs constant monitoring, then you may have what is called a primary health need. In this case, the NHS will take over.

You'll need to go through a long process of assessment, though, unless your condition is deteriorating fast. In that case, a doctor can fast-track you and you'll get a decision within forty-eight hours.

The NHS can also give you a Personal Health Budget, if you have a care package at home. This can allow you to choose and pay your own carer, for instance.

Council help is means tested. You may have to contribute a certain amount from your own finances, depending on the amount of capital you possess. Under present rules, if you have over £23,250 in capital (and this may include the value of your home, unless your partner continues to live there), you will have to pay for a care home place yourself. This is likely to cost anywhere between £600 and £1,200 a week, depending on your needs and where you live.

Unless you have complex or severe health needs, you'll probably be liable to pay. This is not a problem for those who are wealthy enough to simply pay up. It's also not a problem if you live in rented accommodation and have limited savings or income; in this case, the state will pay up. The people who get hit hard by the need to pay for long-term care are those in the middle.

You might think it won't happen to you, but the need for long-term care is high. Recent UK government guidance says that around three out of four adults over sixty-five will need long-term care. That's a very high percentage, and it only refers to those who will have paid-for professional care; people who are cared for by relatives or volunteers aren't included.

However, the Dilnot Commission of 2011 assessed the proportion of over-sixty-fives needing long term care as only one in four. That still means, though, that any couple stand a 50% chance of one of them needing care. You will definitely want to think about how to pay for care. You may also want to talk to a financial advisor about how to protect your partner and your estate from being wiped out by long-term care payments. Taking action well ahead of time can help. However, if you try to move or give away assets once it's clear you'll need care (this is termed 'deprivation of assets'), the government can claim the money back.

Other things to think about

A study by RBC Wealth Management showed that there is a 60% chance of one partner in a couple needing long-term care. It also showed that the average age that they start to need it is as low as sixty-nine – this isn't something that only affects ninety-year-olds. Some people choose family care, while others prefer to be self-funding, but both these strategies come with downsides. Relying on family can lead to fraught relationships and put huge pressure on the 'sandwich carer' who has both parents and children to look after, while self-funding can make planning for capital gains and inheritance difficult.

You might also want to think about what happens if you both need care.

Usually, we think that one of a couple will be able to look after the other, but that's not always the case. Being able to spend the rest of your lives together without being able to look after each other is difficult; planning care for couples can be a very complex issue.

It's difficult, if you're middle aged or even in your sixties (or older!) and in robust health, to imagine a time when you might need help to take a bath, feed yourself, or keep clean. Many people are made very anxious by the idea of losing their independence, and this may make them resist thinking about the issues involved. But having a choice about what kind of care you receive, and where, is often critical to maintaining a good quality of life, so it's worth ensuring you'll have that choice.

Creating your action plan for long-term care

First of all, gauge how likely it is that you will need long-term care. Look at the data (that about half of us need long-term care in retirement), and look at your family's typical longevity, care needs and any hereditary ailments that might come into play.

US

Secondly, work out what long-term care might actually cost you. In 2020, in the US, you would have paid $100,000 a year for a private room in a good nursing home, but costs are very location-specific. Check out Genworth's Cost of Care Survey (https://www.genworth.com/aging-and-you/finances/cost-of-care.html) to see what it's likely to cost where you live.

You might need long-term care for two or three years, although women generally need it for a little longer, as their life expectancy is higher and they tend to outlive their husbands. That means you'd need $200-300,000 in total for your care. Hiring in-home care is cheaper, but of course you will still be paying for your housing costs and can't sell your home to pay for it.

This has possibly given you a bit of a shock. As a third step, you now need to assess how you are going to pay for that care. Will you have enough assets to cover both your living expenses *and* any eventual long-term care? If you know you will have more than enough, then you can probably decide to fund your own care costs, should you need to. But if finances look a bit tight, some kind of insurance is advisable. If your insurance budget is so tight that you can't even afford the insurance, then you'll have to trust Medicaid.

The fourth step, if you've decided to self-fund, is to put those assets in place. If you are still putting together your retirement funds, you could simply increase your contributions to take account of long-term care needs. As you approach retirement, it's best to set up a separate 'bucket' or 'pot' for your care fund. A traditional IRA is probably the best place, because even though you'll pay tax on the income, long-term care is tax deductible in the US, offsetting any tax bills.

If you want to take out insurance, you'll want to decide between a hybrid policy and a stand-alone policy. Stand-alone policies have become less competitive in the last decade, with fewer providers, and higher prices; premiums often rise, giving you the choice of paying a higher premium or giving up the insurance you've already paid for. Over a fifth of applicants aged over fifty are denied coverage because of health issues and that rises to a third of over-sixty-fives. If you can get a stand-alone insurance, though, you can use HSA assets to pay for it. The negative, of course, is that if you never need the insurance, you get nothing out of it.

A hybrid policy may have less strict health screening, and you can buy one for a lump sum, so you won't see the premiums increase. Hybrid policies include long-term care together with either an annuity or a life policy. However, they are more difficult to evaluate than stand-alone policies, making it difficult to comparison shop.

If you can't afford the insurance payments, you need to check the rules on Medicaid. Key issues include the assets you can own while still qualifying – this is particularly difficult if one of a couple needs care while the other stays in the family home. There's also a 'lookback' period for assets transferred to your family.

The main message I want you to get from this chapter is not 'buy insurance' or 'you will need care' – it's just that this is an issue you need to think about. I stress that because a study by Lincoln Financial Group shows that 96% of Americans say it's important to plan for long-term care. How many do you think have actually planned for it? Just 17% – it's too difficult for the others to think about.

UK

Again, as a second step, work out how much it is likely to cost; work out if you're entitled to any state help with care costs using Legal & General's calculator (https://www.legalandgeneral.com/retirement/care/costs-calculator/).

For the third step, think about how you will fund the care. There is currently no long-term health care insurance similar to what exists in the US. However, if you have not yet retired and your health is impaired, you may be able to get a better annuity rate on your pension, which can help pay for care.

Another way to pay for care is to purchase an immediate needs annuity – step four. This will pay out directly towards the cost of your care. Since the money goes to the care provider, it won't count as your income; that means you won't have to pay income tax on it. You'll need to pay a lump sum for the annuity, but it removes the uncertainty of wondering whether your money will run out.

Chapter Twelve
RETIREMENT HACKS

Retirement is a great opportunity, but it can come as something of a shock. One friend of my father's hit the ground running: on day one of retirement, she turned up for her first flying lesson and was able to get her pilot's license aged sixty-one. Another had been looking forward to some 'peace and quiet' after a life of bus and truck driving, but after a month of doing nothing, was going stir crazy. He ended up going back to work as a bus driver and tour guide for a local transport museum.

So while most of this book has been about how to prepare for retirement, this chapter will look at how you cope when you are retired. Some of it is about coping with a lower income, which might take some adjustment, and some of it is about coping with a different lifestyle and different priorities.

Some tips for retirement

Get rid of your debt

Ensure if you can that your mortgage, car loans and any credit card debt is paid off before you retire. That will free up your income for actually living on rather than paying lenders their interest.

If you can't do this out of cash flow, it might be worth selling some assets to get there. You might decide to sell your home and buy a smaller place. If you have two cars, or a car and a pickup, selling one might pay off the loan on the other. That's not going to be an easy decision to take, but it could dramatically improve your lifestyle.

Avoid big commitments

If you look at all your monthly and annual subscriptions, they may be taking up a large amount of your income; gym, cable TV, phone, internet, clubs, sports facilities, magazines, and so on can build up.

And avoid taking on new commitments, too. A lot of scammers know that retirees can make good targets. It's worth taking the time to read up on the latest scams; some of them are very clever. Don't think "It won't be me, I'm wised up." CEOs and even the French foreign minister have been taken in by deepfake video scams. In the UK, a lot of scammers have 'sure-fire investments' and 'high-return funds' to sell to retirees who may have taken a lump sum out of their pension fund; some sound very plausible.

And don't splurge in your first year or two. It's tempting to take a cruise or buy an RV, but unless your retirement is really well funded, it's much wiser to see how you are managing your budgets first. Then you'll know just how much leeway you have for spending on your big dreams.

Reduce your household bills

Once you retire (if you haven't already done so), try to find cheaper suppliers (that includes insurance), and do a quick energy-efficiency audit. LED light bulbs, better insulation, and so on, can make a big difference. Your energy bills may go up if you have gone from the daily commute to being at home all day, so think about when you need heating or air conditioning and find ways to limit the bill. For example, this might involve not heating rooms you don't use often, using less hot water in the shower, or getting smart multiple sockets so you can switch all your computer or home entertainment devices off at the same time.

Prioritize or trim your bucket list

Okay, if you want to climb Kilimanjaro, do it sooner rather than later in retirement, while you're in good health and fighting fit. But you might, for instance, have both India and Japan on your list; India is a *lot* cheaper. If you want to go hiking and kayaking, hiking doesn't require a kayak, some way of getting it to the river, and instructions, just good boots and rainproofs and a map and compass.

A bucket list has a tendency to grow and grow and grow. Go through it and pick the things you absolutely don't want to compromise on and the things that can wait. Even if you have way more income than you need (unusual, but it happens), you don't have unlimited time, so choose the things that are most important to you.

Retire in a less expensive environment

Do this and you can stretch your income and funds much further. If your children have all left home and you have a six-bedroom house, you might not need it and can move to a smaller property. Or maybe you have to live near your work in London, New York or San Francisco, but in retirement, you could move much further away to where real estate and living costs are cheaper. You could even move to a different country, but if you want to do that, you'll need to check that you qualify for a visa if one is needed. One way of doing this is through a golden visa; in exchange for a donation or investment in business or real estate, you will be offered a visa to live in the country without the normal requirements. For example, St Lucia offer golden visas for those who make a minimum $100,000 donation. Portugal offers a golden visa for those that invest a minimum of €280,000 into real estate. Some other countries offering golden visas in return for donations or investment include Greece, Malta, Grenada and Montenegro. Just think, you could be living your retirement by the beach, just as you always dreamed.

Of course, if you sell an expensive house or flat, you may end up with some extra capital as well as lower costs – a double whammy.

Actively look for lower prices and senior offers

If tax reliefs, lower-cost memberships, or senior citizen discounts are available, make sure you take advantage (sometimes, if you're quite youthful looking, you won't be offered them, so you need to ask!). In the UK, you should get a winter fuel allowance; it won't pay all your bills, but it's useful income none the less. Some shops, cafes and restaurants have 'senior specials' and these can be very welcome if your retirement income has proved a little less than generous.

Plan your healthcare costs

Just because you're in great form right now doesn't mean you will always stay healthy. Basic Medicare is not enough for most, so make sure you have supplementary insurance. Also, ensure you have local support from family or friends should you become unable to drive or need to have pets looked after while you are in hospital. Sorting things out *before* they happen is very helpful and avoids stress and worry.

Remember that things can change

You need to have some contingency plans in place. A recession, stock market crash, or new tax rules could impact your retirement income. You may need to change your priorities. Might family members need help if, for instance, they're laid off, or grandchildren can't afford to buy a home?

Don't idle away your retirement

Nowadays, life expectancy after retirement can be as much as thirty years. Do you really want to spend it watching daytime TV and doing sudoku? Keep active, whether you're volunteering in community projects, working part-time, getting involved in sport, traveling, or just seeing lots of your friends and family. I know one oldie of ninety-something who loves gardening and wildlife and has turned her garden into a project laboratory for the local school. Last I heard, the children were coming around to make insect hotels and bat boxes!

Remember that being happy isn't about being perfect

If you've worked in business, you may have come across Maslow's 'hierarchy of needs.' First comes just surviving – getting enough to eat, having a home. Then comes the need for security – if you have a regular retirement income, you're a lot of the way there. Then you need love and belonging, which might be your family, or your sports team, or your community, or all of those.

Once these are met, you can go on to the need for esteem – something that's difficult for retirees who were used to getting their sense of self-worth from their careers. So that's something that might be missing, and you'll need to find new ways of getting it. Finally, there's what Maslow calls 'self-actualization,' or you might call it 'living your best life.'

So you need to think about what's really important to you. And be honest. It's easy to say "of course, it's my family" – which is great, if you're getting fulfillment out of helping teach your grandchildren math, having holidays with your kids, and so on. But is it? What do you *need* to live your best life? Intellectual stimulation? Manual work? Creating things? Adrenalin? Music?

Would you rather spend a few thousand on a cello, a top-notch road bike, a trip to Europe, or a beaten-up pick-up truck? (There is no right answer).

There are actually studies that say that beyond a certain limit, you get diminishing returns from wealth. Researchers at Princeton found that people feel happier the more they make, but only up to $75,000 – then, their happiness plateaus and more money doesn't bring more happiness. So try to focus on the things that are going to make you happy rather than on the level of income you have.

Stay positive

Being in retirement can feel like you are in death's waiting room, particularly when Facebook keeps sending you ads for incontinence pads and funeral plans. In fact, when you retire, you've got twenty or thirty years of life still ahead of you.

You may also look back on your career or on your life generally and regret some of the choices you made. "It's too late to fix it," you say to yourself.

But retirement is not time to give up on your life. Sure, you may never get the Pulitzer or Nobel Prize, but you can still achieve things. You might have always wanted to write a history of your local fire service, chart the development of your city through the years, or learn another language. My grandfather learned German in his sixties and Turkish in his seventies. You might suddenly find an opportunity that opens your eyes to a whole new area of life. President Carter in his nineties was helping build houses for low-income families and you could see from photos how much he loved building something. Other people have suddenly found a spiritual guru or started to work in the arts or in theater, perhaps through a chance meeting.

If, by the way, you actually are depressed once you retire (and this does happen to quite a few people in retirement), then seek medical help or therapy. Above all, don't spend your time in denial. Low energy, pessimistic thoughts, and poor motivation are usually signs that something is wrong, so get help fixing it.

Keep control of your cash flow

Doing a cash flow analysis will show you where your money is coming from and where it's going. There are plenty of good tools online, or, if you have a financial advisor, you may want to sit down with them to go through the process. Remember that your needs may change over time as you grow older. You may have a more active lifestyle right after you retire, but ten years later, you may be less active and more of a homebody.

You should look at both sides of the equation. For instance, if you have one poorly performing investment, you might want to consider changing it. You might want to see if, for instance, you can get better returns on your cash by making a fixed-term deposit or using a CD ladder. And you should check what repairs and maintenance are costing on your car and home, as well as your other outgoings. Sometimes replacing a car or a heating system can be cheaper than continuing to pay high repair bills (particularly if you can replace it with a more energy-efficient model).

Set your investment strategy

Work out the blend of investments you need. It's often said that retirees should not have any equity or real estate holdings, but that's advice that comes down from the past when retirees didn't live very long after retirement. You may have thirty years ahead, so don't risk inflation destroying your assets and income. However, you will want to balance a portfolio of reasonably conservative investments. Retirement isn't the right time to start investing in jatropha plantations, Russian equities or cryptocurrencies (if you want to dabble in cryptocurrencies, treat it as a hobby, and your 'investment' as spending on your leisure interests, just like a golf club subscription).

Make sure you monitor your strategy regularly to ensure it's still up to date, as well as monitoring its performance. For instance, if you have direct holdings in property, even if they're highly profitable, at some point you might want to swap them for property funds like REITs in order to simplify your life.

If anything's tax free, it's worth having

For instance, in the UK, you can take 25% of your total pension savings as a tax-free lump sum. That's worth having. You can invest it probably at better rates than an annuity would give you, and it's there in future if you have extra costs that your regular income doesn't cover.

If you're planning to retire abroad, check out your tax status. For instance, Portugal only taxes pension and investment income at 10% when you move there.

And there's a special hack if you have a 401k and change job after age fifty-five. You can take your money out of your 401k without paying the IRS early withdrawal penalty. But if you roll it into your IRA, you'll have to pay the penalty when you take the money out. On the other hand, if you get a new job, you can roll the whole 401k into a new one, even if you only work there a few weeks – and there will be no early retirement penalty once you leave.

Have a plan B

Your plans are probably for a long and enjoyable retirement. Life may have other things in store. Have a plan for what you can do if your health takes a turn for the worse, or if one of your investments goes bad, or if you need to go into sheltered accommodation. If you move state or country, have a re-entry plan in case you find your new home doesn't match up to expectations. Your plan B needn't be a terribly detailed plan, but you do need to have one.

Check out your inheritance tax/estate tax status

Also check whether pension assets can be transferred to your beneficiaries (note that usually you will have to do this directly with the pension provider as your pension assets don't form part of your estate). Take any action that's necessary, such as giving money to your family in advance, or setting up trusts (which we covered earlier).

Conclusion

Whether you're reading this book to find out how to save for a retirement that's still forty years away or to catch up on your retirement planning in your fifties, I hope you have found some useful information that you can act on.

A lot of people I know treated retirement as something that was just going to look after itself. One day, they would get the gold watch and the pension, and then they were just going to be retired people, just like one day you're a kid and then in a while you find you've become a teenager. But it's not like that. If you really want a good retirement, you'll need to take on responsibility for thinking what you want your retirement to look like, what that's going to cost and how you're going to pay for it.

You're probably fed up with hearing me say this, but one more time I *will* say it: the earlier you start saving and investing, the better retirement you will have. You don't have to put the money in a pension fund or a 401k or IRA (though these come with tax advantages); you can choose other investments, like rental property, or shares held in an ISA. But you do need to get your investments working for you, as social security is very unlikely to be enough.

It's also a great idea, well before you retire, to think about what you really want to do with your life in retirement. It might be restoring an old watermill. It might be playing poker. It might be finally getting around to doing a degree in archeology, or traveling the world, or painting oil portraits of all your friends. And it *might* be being a homebody, seeing the grandchildren every weekend, and doing some gardening.

The more self-knowledge you have, and the more rooted you are in the values that underpin your life, the more likely you are to enjoy the best retirement ever.

If you enjoyed this book and found it valuable, I would be really grateful if you would consider leaving a review. Your feedback is incredibly valuable and helps other readers discover and appreciate the book and encourages my writing journey.

References and Further Reading

Books

Birken, E. G. The 5 Years Before You Retire, Updated Edition: Retirement Planning When You Need It the Most.
Simon & Schuster, 2013.

Block, R. L. Investing in REITs: Real Estate Investment Trusts.
Wiley, 1998.

Bogle, J. C. Bogle on Mutual Funds: New Perspectives For The Intelligent Investor.
Wiley, 2015.

Ferri, R. The ETF Book: All You Need To Know About Exchange-Traded Funds
Wiley, 2009.

Fisker, J. L. Early Retirement Extreme: A Philosophical and Practical Guide to Financial Independence.
CreateSpace, 2010.

Guilarducci, T. How To Retire With Enough Money: And How to Know

What Enough Is.
Workman Publishing Company, 2015.

Pfau, W. D. Retirement Planning Guidebook: Navigating the Important Decisions for Retirement Success.
Retirement Researcher Media, 2021.

Krewson-Kelly, S. The Intelligent REIT Investor.
Wiley, 2016.

Quinn, J. B. How to Make Your Money Last: The Indispensable Retirement Guide.
Simon & Schuster, 2020.

Rieckens, S. Playing with FIRE (Financial Independence Retire Early): How Far Would You Go for Financial Freedom?
New World Library, 2019.

Scott, J. The Book on Flipping Houses.
BiggerPockets, 2013.

Turner, B. The Book on Rental Property Investing.
BiggerPockets, 2015.

Tyson, E. Mutual Funds for Dummies.
Wiley, 1998.

Wychcote, J. Your Little Book of Asset Allocation.
Everything You Need for Worry-Free Investment. 2022.

Courses

The Yale Happiness Course: The Science of Well-Being.
https://www.coursera.org/learn/the-science-of-well-being (free)

Web articles

https://www.evelyn.com/media/c3fgf0jw/route-2-evelyn-partners-retirement-campaign-e-guide-jun-22-final.pdf

https://www.thebalancemoney.com/best-retirement-strategies-for-your-20s-417758

https://www.cnbc.com/2019/12/12/system-is-flawed-when-most-americans-have-tiny-retirement-savings.html

https://www.thebalancemoney.com/what-is-retirement-2388822

https://www.plsa.co.uk/Policy-and-Research/Topics/State-pension-reform#:~:text=Key%20facts,subject%20to%20a%20means%20test

https://news.calpers.ca.gov/learn-the-4-phases-of-retirement/#:~:text=In%20fact%2C%20there%20are%20generally,and%20lifestyle%20needs%20more%20thoroughly

https://www.boringmoney.co.uk/learn/articles/pension-prep-5-things-to-do-when-nearing-retirement/

https://money.usnews.com/money/blogs/on-retirement/articles/2018-09-13/7-surprising-ways-retirement-will-change-your-life

https://www.cnbc.com/2022/05/16/americans-can-expect-to-pay-a-lot-more-for-medical-care-in-retirement.html

https://ncoa.org/article/top-5-financial-scams-targeting-older-adults#:~:text=Financial%20scams%20targeting%20older%20adults%20are%20costly%2C%20widespread%2C%20and%20on,in%20losses%20compared%20to%202020.

https://www.cnbc.com/2022/10/24/more-americans-live-paycheck-to-paycheck-as-inflation-outpaces-income.html

https://www.pwc.com/us/en/industries/financial-services/library/retirement-in-america.html

https://www.pwc.com/us/en/industries/asset-wealth-management/assets/pwc-retirement-in-america-rethink-retool.pdf

https://www.geneveinvest.com/avoidable-mistakes-retirement/

https://www.fool.com/investing/2021/09/22/should-you-stash-retirement-funds-in-bank-accounts/

https://www.forbes.com/sites/ebauer/2022/01/05/do-retirees-have-too-much-risk-and-whose-fault-is-that/?sh=57f4fd341949

https://sponsor.fidelity.com/bin-public/06_PSW_Website/documents/Building_Financial_Futures.pdf

https://www.forbes.com/advisor/retirement/retirement-planning-how-to-get-out-of-debt-before-retirement/

https://www.moneyhelper.org.uk/en/pensions-and-retirement/tax-and-pensions/a-guide-to-tax-in-retirement

https://www.finra.org/investors/learn-to-invest/types-investments/retirement/managing-retirement-income/taxation-retirement-income

https://thepeoplespension.co.uk/media-centre/press-releases/retirement-crisis-predicted/

https://thepeoplespension.co.uk/downloads/xx-tpp-1710-0722-pension-adequacy-report-v6/

https://www.weforum.org/agenda/2022/06/frequency-pay-financial-well-being/

https://yourdivorcequestions.org/how-will-divorce-affect-me-financially/

https://rethinking65.com/2022/02/18/gambling-addictions-threaten-retirement-plans/

https://www.verywellhealth.com/do-crossword-puzzles-prevent-dementia

https://www.health.harvard.edu/mind-and-mood/protecting-against-cognitive-decline

https://retirement.fidelity.co.uk/news-insights/financial-wellness/financial-wellness/saving-and-spending-rule-thumb/

https://www.nerdwallet.com/article/finance/best-budget-apps https://monzo.com/blog/envelope-method-budgeting

https://goodbudget.com/envelope-budgeting/

https://www.phoenixlife.co.uk/retirement-centre/what-can-i-expect-to-receive-in-retirement/annual-retirement-budget-planner

https://www.blackrock.com/us/individual/education/retirement/building-a-retirement-budget

https://www.boringmoney.co.uk/learn/learning-paths/pension-planners/

https://www.boringmoney.co.uk/learn/articles/pension-prep-5-things-to-do-in-accumulation/ -

https://www.boringmoney.co.uk/learn/articles/pension-prep-5-things-to-do-in-pre-retirement/ -

https://www.usa.gov/about-social-security#:-:text=Social%20Security%20provides%20you%20with,the%20event%20of%20your%20death.

https://www.ssa.gov/benefits/retirement/

https://www.investopedia.com/articles/taxes/11/tax-deferred-tax-exempt.asp

https://www.dol.gov/general/topic/retirement/typesofplans

https://www.investopedia.com/ask/answers/102714/how-are-simplified-employee-pension-sep-iras-taxed.asp

https://www.investopedia.com/retirement/401k-contribution-limits/

https://www.irs.gov/retirement-plans/retirement-plans-faqs-regarding-403b-tax-sheltered-annuity-plans

https://retirable.com/advice/retirement-accounts/retirement-savings:-tax-deferred-or-tax-exempt

https://www.irs.gov/retirement-plans/retirement-plans-faqs-regarding-required-minimum-distributions

https://www.gov.uk/employers-workplace-pensions-rules

https://www.ageuk.org.uk/information-advice/money-legal/pensions/workplace-pensions/

https://www.litrg.org.uk/tax-guides/tax-basics/do-i-have-join-pension-scheme/do-you-know-how-tax-relief-your-pension

https://www.investor.gov/additional-resources/retirement-toolkit/employer-sponsored-plans/employee-stock-ownership-plans

https://www.nerdwallet.com/article/investing/index-funds-vs-mutual-funds

https://www.investopedia.com/terms/i/indexfund.asp

https://www.investopedia.com/terms/m/mutualfund.asp

https://www.mandg.com/pru/customer/en-gb/guides/investments/types/investment-bonds

https://www.investopedia.com/terms/g/government-bond.asp

https://www.investopedia.com/terms/r/reig.asp

https://www.investopedia.com/terms/r/reit.asp

https://www.investor.gov/introduction-investing/investing-basics/investment-products/insurance-products/annuities

https://www.usbank.com/retirement-planning/open-an-ira/what-is-an-ira.html

https://www.firstrepublic.com/insights-education/average-american-debt

https://www.forbes.com/advisor/retirement/seniors-debt-statistics/

https://www.fool.com/the-ascent/credit-cards/articles/67-of-retirees-have-credit-card-debt-3-steps-to-pay-it-off-on-a-fixed-income/

https://www.rbcwealthmanagement.com/en-us/insights/the-real-cost-of-health-care-in-retirement

https://www.investopedia.com/financial-edge/0710/5-ways-debt-can-make-you-money.aspx

https://www.finra.org/investors/learn-to-invest/types-investments/retirement/managing-retirement-income/taxation-retirement-income

https://www.investopedia.com/articles/personal-finance/101514/power-attorney-do-you-need-one.asp

https://www.legalzoom.com/articles/transferring-assets-into-a-living-trust-can-you-do-it-yourself

https://www.investopedia.com/terms/q/qualified-personal-residence-trust.asp

https://www.investopedia.com/terms/q/qtip.asp

https://www.investopedia.com/terms/c/charitableleadtrust.asp

https://www.blufftonsun.com/why-its-necessary-to-consider-using-separate-share-trusts/

https://www.investopedia.com/terms/b/blindtrust.asp

https://www.investopedia.com/terms/s/special-needs-trust.asp

https://www.investopedia.com/terms/c/creditsheltertrust.asp

https://www.investopedia.com/terms/g/generation-skippingtrust.asp

https://www.investopedia.com/terms/i/insurance_trust.asp

https://www.standardlife.co.uk/articles/article-page/reasons-to-pay-your-pension-some-attention

https://www.ncbi.nlm.nih.gov/books/NBK148839/

https://www.divorcenet.com/resources/common-reasons-marriages-end.html

https://osf.io/preprints/socarxiv/h2sk6/

https://www.johnhancock.com/ideas-insights/reasons-to-prioritize-saving-for-retirement.html

https://www.mycnote.com/

https://www.greenamerica.org/social-investing

https://thegiin.org/impact-investing/need-to-know/#what-is-impact-investing

https://investingreviews.co.uk/blog/why-do-online-banks-have-higher-interest-rates/

https://www.bankrate.com/uk/savings-accounts/how-to-create-a-passive-income-stream/

https://www.forbes.com/uk/advisor/investing/best-passive-income-ideas/

https://www.propertypartner.co/what-is-property-crowdfunding

https://www.simplecrowdfunding.co.uk/news/what-is-crowdfunding

https://www.investopedia.com/articles/mortgages-real-estate/08/house-flip.asp

https://www.investopedia.com/articles/mortgages-real-estate/08/house-flip.asp

https://www.fortunebuilders.com/a-beginners-guide-to-buy-hold-real-estate/

https://www.reit.com/what-reit

https://www.forbes.com/advisor/investing/best-real-estate-etf/

https://www.investopedia.com/articles/investing/090815/buying-your-first-investment-property-top-10-tips.asp

https://www.weforum.org/agenda/2022/01/online-learning-courses-reskill-skills-gap/

https://thrivethemes.com/how-to-teach-online/

https://malwarwickonbooks.com/americans-read-books/

https://www.investopedia.com/terms/a/affiliate-marketing.asp

https://www.investopedia.com/terms/m/multi-level-marketing.asp

https://www.investopedia.com/terms/d/dividend.asp

https://www.financial-expert.co.uk/how-to-become-a-business-angel-investor-uk/

https://swoopfunding.com/uk/equity-financing/seis-vs-eis-explained-whats-the-difference/

https://www.investopedia.com/terms/s/seedcapital.asp

https://study.com/academy/lesson/public-equity-funds-definition-structure.htm

https://www.investopedia.com/articles/investing/030415/difference-between-private-and-public-equity.asp

https://www.shopify.com/uk/blog/become-an-entrepreneur

https://www.simplypsychology.org/maslow.html

https://bestinterest.blog/the-fulfillment-curve/

https://www.cnbc.com/2021/01/22/new-wharton-study-people-are-happier-when-they-earn-more-money.html

https://www.boringmoney.co.uk/learn/articles/pension-prep-5-things-to-do-in-drawdown/

https://www.investopedia.com/terms/i/inheritancetax.asp

https://investor.vanguard.com/investor-resources-education/retirement/planning-long-term-care

https://www.genworth.com/aging-and-you/finances/cost-of-care.html

https://www.morningstar.com/articles/932642/an-action-plan-for-long-term-care

https://www.kiplinger.com/retirement/long-term-care/603422/is-your-retirement-plan-missing-an-essential-piece

https://www.sciencedaily.com/releases/2022/09/220912163802.htm

https://www.unbiased.co.uk/news/financial-adviser/one-in-six-over-55s-have-no-pension-savings-yet

https://www.forbes.com/advisor/retirement/the-forbes-guide-to-fire/

https://www.investopedia.com/terms/f/financial-independence-retire-early-fire.asp

https://www.businessnewsdaily.com/15252-what-is-the-fire-movement.html

https://www.thetimes.co.uk/money-mentor/article/how-to-retire-early-the-fire-method/

https://www.thisismoney.co.uk/money/pensions/article-11723481/FIRE-followers-retire-40-years-frugality-8-rules.html

https://moneymountaingoat.com/types-of-fire/

https://www.nytimes.com/2019/06/07/business/fire-women-retire-early.html

Made in the USA
Las Vegas, NV
21 July 2023

75043054R00083